P9-CRT-722

Unlocking Public Value

Unlocking Public Value

A NEW MODEL FOR ACHIEVING HIGH PERFORMANCE IN PUBLIC SERVICE ORGANIZATIONS

Martin Cole

and

Greg Parston

John Wiley & Sons, Inc.

Copyright © 2006 by Accenture LLP. All rights reserved.

Published by John Wiley & Sons, Inc., Hoboken, New Jersey.
Published simultaneously in Canada.

No part of this publication may be reproduced, stored in a retrieval system, or transmitted in any form or by any means, electronic, mechanical, photocopying, recording, scanning, or otherwise, except as permitted under Section 107 or 108 of the 1976 United States Copyright Act, without either the prior written permission of the Publisher, or authorization through payment of the appropriate per-copy fee to the Copyright Clearance Center, Inc., 222 Rosewood Drive, Danvers, MA 01923, (978) 750-8400, fax (978) 646-8600, or on the Web at www.copyright.com. Requests to the Publisher for permission should be addressed to the Permissions Department, John Wiley & Sons, Inc., 111 River Street, Hoboken, NJ 07030, (201) 748-6011, fax (201) 748-6008, or online at http://www.wiley.com/go/permissions.

Limit of Liability/Disclaimer of Warranty: While the publisher and author have used their best efforts in preparing this book, they make no representations or warranties with respect to the accuracy or completeness of the contents of this book and specifically disclaim any implied warranties of merchantability or fitness for a particular purpose. No warranty may be created or extended by sales representatives or written sales materials. The advice and strategies contained herein may not be suitable for your situation. You should consult with a professional where appropriate. Neither the publisher nor author shall be liable for any loss of profit or any other commercial damages, including but not limited to special, incidental, consequential, or other damages.

Wiley also publishes its books in a variety of electronic formats. Some content that appears in print may not be available in electronic books. For more information about Wiley products, visit our Web site at www.wiley.com.

Library of Congress Cataloging-in-Publication Data:

Cole, Martin, 1956–
Unlocking public value : a new model for achieving high performance in public service organizations / Marty Cole and Greg Parston.
p. cm.
Includes bibliographical references.
ISBN-13: 978-0-471-95945-8
ISBN-10: 0-471-95945-6 (cloth)

1. Government productivity—Evaluation. 2. Public administration. I. Parston, Gregory. II. Title.
JF1525.P67C65 2006
352.3—dc22

2006011222

Printed in the United States of America.

10 9 8 7 6 5 4 3

For Vivienne Jupp, whose vision for this book and
active participation made it happen.

Contents

Introduction

Among the many admirable aims of the environmental movement, the one that strikes me as most useful to those in public services is captured by the motto, "Think globally, act locally." In a public services career spanning more than 35 years, I have had a chance to look at public service systems in the Americas, Europe and Africa. I have been forcibly struck by the need to give substantial weight to the local political and cultural context of a particular system. You ignore a genuine understanding of these features at your peril: You, the public services administrator or elected official, must be seen to listen and pay attention to local priorities. In other words, act locally. At the same time, my experience in South Africa and Canada (which in key ways face vastly different challenges) and elsewhere is that there are some major global economic, human and social drivers that all politicians and public service administrators need to take account of in their engagement with their citizens. Think globally.

In *Unlocking Public Value,* Marty Cole and Greg Parston offer public services practitioners a unique tool to help them capture the mix of goals or outcomes, some reflecting local, some global, concerns, and measure performance in attaining these outcomes. Providing a framework and step-by-step process for defining these outcomes is one of the key achievements of the book. Since nearly all meaningful outcomes come at a cost to taxpayers, the measuring of outcomes occurs in the context of tracking not just costs, but cost-effectiveness as well.

Following are some of the critical questions that I have found over the years underlie successful approaches to delivering public services around the world:

- How do you improve the quality of public services?
- How do you hold down the tax bill for public services, as few societies willingly agree to pay more?

- How do you achieve value for money that is credible to citizens?
- What role could the private sector play to add skills and experience?
- How do you involve public service workers without allowing their needs to overdominate?

Citizen-Centric

Implicit in these questions is the goal of putting the citizen at the center of all efforts to provide and improve upon public services. Most public service leaders and administrators at least give lip service to putting the citizen first. However, it is frustrating, but not surprising, to find that competing interests vie with those of citizens time and again in locales around the world. Attempts to maintain the public service status quo among various interests too often has the effect of slighting citizens' needs, despite the best of stated intentions.

A model for public services centered on the citizen is depicted in simplified form by the following diagram. As indicated in the above questions, the citizen wants more and better public services without bearing a greater tax burden. Those desires drive dynamic relationships with the other four public service "players" described below, including elected officials, managers and administrators, public service workers and public-private sector partnerships. In many cases these four groups also interact with each other at various times, of course, but I have resisted the temptation to create a cat's cradle of criss-crossing lines and arrows.

Politicians and managers and administrators must establish trust in their leadership if they are to succeed in effectively providing public value. Time and again I have found in different societies that politicians and managers struggle to establish this trust. Politicians frequently want quick results and pay less attention to long-term needs. Managers fail to accept the real pressure the politicians work under. Successful public service strategies need to

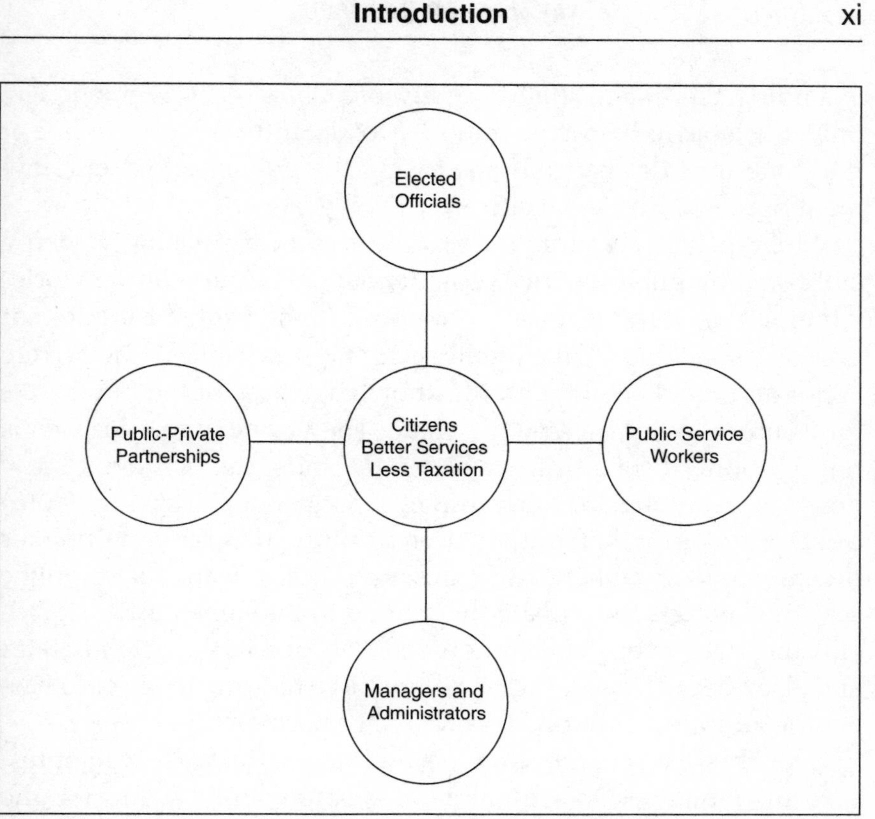

incorporate both of these aspects so that there can be an integrated political/managerial response to the needs of the citizen. Politicians and managers need to take the time and effort to involve local citizens in setting goals and clearly set out the strategies that will be followed to achieve those goals.

Addressing the concerns of public service workers and related groups in the context of a citizen-focused approach to providing public services is one of the biggest challenges facing public service leaders. In Canada, where most public service systems are regarded as working fairly well, it has been my experience that some systems staff, accustomed to the strong influence of trade unions, have resisted the transition to a more citizen-centric approach. And in South Africa the public sector is struggling with extending the quantity and quality of public services previously only available to the white minority to all South Africans, while at the same time dramatically increasing the public service employment opportunities to all citizens.

Public-private sector partnerships are increasingly being embraced by public service providers in many parts of the world. Although the trend is most pronounced in the United Kingdom, it is clearly spreading as the public sector taps the skills of the private sector and melds them with the knowledge base of the public sector in order to enhance public value. The partnership approach is not without difficulties, however. Despite the United States' deserved reputation as the leading proponent of private sector efficiencies and growth, there has been a failure in the competition for procurement of public services in several cases. Many major public service contracts are repeatedly granted to the same parties at federal and state levels. More emphasis is needed in the United States and elsewhere on encouraging competitive bidding in order to hasten the adoption of public-private sector partnerships.

Over the next several years it is a virtual certainty that the pressure in public services to provide greater public value for the money being spent will only increase. *Unlocking Pubic Value* is an important step in addressing what the authors refer to as this "value squeeze." Applying the concept of private sector shareholder value to the public sector, with citizens substituting for shareholders in broad terms, gives the public services participant a fresh approach to the challenges he or she faces. At the same time it keeps citizen concerns at the center of attempts to balance social outcomes and cost-effectiveness. And that is right where citizen concerns belong, regardless of whether you are thinking globally or acting locally.

Sir Andrew Foster
Chief Executive of the
Audit Commission for
England and Wales
1992–2003

Preface

A group restructuring Ontario's health care system is feeling it. So are the heads of Spain's social security system and the directors of a prestigious cultural institution in downtown Tokyo. Public managers around the world, in fact, are under increasing pressure to do more with less. They are caught in a "value squeeze" as they seek more efficient ways to create public outcomes while stakeholders ranging from legislators to taxpayers to service recipients demand better, faster service.

In the twenty-first century, public managers are increasingly seeking ways to help them "do more with less" and to answer critical questions about public sector productivity: Are we spending public money as cost-effectively as possible? Are the taxes spent creating the public outcomes that taxpayers want? Our goal in introducing the Public Service Value Model is to give public managers a framework to use to answer these and other questions crucial to their quest to act in the public interest.

An Indicator of Public Value

If public service organizations want to demonstrate the value they are bringing to the public and to show how effectively they are spending taxpayer money, what tools and frameworks are available for their use? Unlike the private sector that has widely understood metrics like profitability and a stock market with publicly available company performance information, there are no universally accepted standards for measuring and assessing value in the public sector. The Accenture Public Service Value Model[1] adapts some of the core concepts of private sector shareholder value analysis to fill a critical need in the public sector for a rigorous way of defining, measuring and improving performance. At its core, the Public Service Value Model is designed to help public managers eager to answer two fundamental questions about public service organizations and their programs: Why (or to what end) does this organization or program exist? And, how will we know when the organization or program has achieved its intended purpose or goal?

One central argument in this book is that public managers who clearly and consistently articulate the intended outcomes of their organizations and programs and then measure their progress in achieving those outcomes will go a long way toward making their organization accountable in the eyes of the public and improving their performance over time. The Public Service Value Model is a simple framework that demonstrates the results of public service organizations in a way that stakeholders, such as citizens, taxpayers and public service recipients, can appreciate.

The methodology also has benefits for organizations that use it as a management tool. If the leaders of a public service organization concisely and repeatedly articulate the organization's outcomes, as well as recognize when its goals are achieved, it is likely that employees will more easily understand how their work ties into the greater public good that the organization is intended to produce. If public managers have this discipline, their organizations can increasingly focus on the most important tasks and align their efforts around key social outcomes.

The goal of the Public Service Value Model is to have a meaningful, relatively easy-to-use way of defining, measuring and increasing the value delivered by public service. For the purpose of this book, our definition of *public service* is meant to be inclusive and to encompass all organizations that are engaged in delivering services to the public that are, at least in part, paid for or underwritten by taxpayer money. Public service organizations include government agencies, which are still the primary providers of public services, but also an increasing number of nonprofit organizations and private sector companies that provide services—usually under contract—that have traditionally been delivered directly by governments. In every country, the determination of what is a public service and of what kinds of organizations provide it is, of course, ultimately a political one. Around the world, though, there is greater diversity and plurality in what traditionally was called simply "the public sector."

Since the first extensive client application in 2003, the Public Service Value Model has been used to help more than 30 public service organizations in Europe, Asia and North America on their journey to high performance. The model has been further modified based on valuable input from many in academia and public service.

Past as Prologue

A great many theories, stretching back nearly a half century, have been devoted to measuring and improving public performance and defining public value. Yet the lack of agreed standards for defining and achieving value in the public sector is one of the key missing links in the public service value chain.

What, after all, comprises high performance in a social services agency, for example, and from whose vantage point can one rate such performance? Social outcomes tend to be harder to define and achieve than outputs, and many public service organizations primarily measure outputs. One of the innovations of the methodology is that it gives public stakeholders a way to define and measure outcomes and answer, "What determines high performance?"

Since the 1990s, government performance measurement mandates, originating with ground-breaking legislation and policies in the United States, the United Kingdom, Canada and France, have spread around much of the world with mixed results. Our approach attempts to build upon the leading theories in the fields of public management and public value and to introduce a practical methodology that public managers can use to put many of these theories of public value into practice.

Introducing the Public Service Value Model

Our goal in introducing the Public Service Value Model, which is being taught at a handful of public policy schools around the world, is to produce a hands-on tool that public managers can apply to meet their needs. The Public Service Value Model is designed to produce results that can be interpreted by various public service stakeholders, including taxpayers and legislators, who are interested in improving their ability to judge how cost-effectively tax revenues are being spent. It is not intended to be an all-or-nothing methodology to replace previous approaches to performance management, such as the Balanced Scorecard or government performance assessments, but rather to be complementary to existing performance management frameworks.

The Public Service Value Model adapts the principles of commercial shareholder value analysis to a public service context, using citizens, the taxpayers and public service recipients as the primary stakeholder. The model considers two levers of "citizen value": outcomes and cost-effectiveness. An outcome is an end result, not to be confused with outputs, that are specific products or services delivered. Broadly speaking, a public service organization generates public value when it delivers a set of social and economic outcomes that are aligned to citizen priorities in a cost-effective manner. By increasing either outcomes or cost-effectiveness, an organization creates value. By increasing one at the expense of the other, an organization makes a trade-off between the two fundamental means of creating value. A decrease in both levers represents a clear reduction in public value.

One of the reporting tools of the Public Service Value Model is a matrix that can enable managers to plot outcomes against cost-effectiveness. Plotting these measures over time allows managers to trace the path of a public service organization's performance and to determine whether it is creating public value, meaning that the organization is achieving a high level of outcomes cost-effectively.

Public managers can use the Public Service Value Model to "tell the performance story" of their organization. The methodology can be used to help public service organizations review their performance and identify practical steps to achieve their performance goals. The model does not focus on inputs such as the number of nurses, teachers or police officers in service. Rather, it is about social outcomes, such as the health of patients, the quality of people's education or the level of public safety.

While the Public Service Value methodology can help identify specific areas of low or high performance through its analysis, it cannot tell us why an organization or sector is doing well or poorly. To understand what is driving performance, we need to conduct a deeper analysis of public service value and investigate what factors are underpinning or contributing to fluctuations in performance. The real strength of the Public Service Value Model is in its demonstration of whether an organization is doing better or worse than in other years, and whether its performance in a given year is better than the average performance over a specified period of time. But, further research and analysis is required to understand the underlying value drivers.

Contrary to many public sector performance measurement approaches that remain vague or imprecise on relating outcomes and expenditures, the Public Service Value Model brings these two key components together to help public managers solve their most pressing problems. The model tracks a handful of key outcomes, weighted in terms of importance, and their cost-effectiveness relative to the organization's average performance over time. Steve Kelman, Weatherhead Professor of Public Management, John F. Kennedy School of Government, Harvard University, noted that what sets this model apart "is the Public Service Value Model's effort to relate results to costs and to track that relationship over time. That is the new thing that the Public Service Value Model brings to the table." The Chief of the Programs Group for a division of the U.S. National Security Agency added, "The process of clarifying our mission, core functions and metrics is critical for us to improve our performance going forward. The Public Service Value Model provided a unique structured approach and the focus we needed to get this effort done." Elliott Hibbs, former Commissioner of the Arizona Department of Revenue, who retired from the agency in April 2005, cut straight to the "bottom line" in his appraisal. He termed the Public Service Value Model "the best advancement I've seen in performance measurement in the last 20 years of my career."

Unlocking Public Value is written with the needs of the "time-starved" public service manager in mind. The first three chapters, of particular interest to generalists and newcomers to the field, address the need for public value and the historical trends that have shaped the pursuit of value in the Americas, Europe and, more recently, Asia. The next three chapters present a detailed "how-to" guide on applying the model, with real-world examples of those who have grappled with unlocking the value of their public service organizations. The final chapter addresses the importance of focusing on innovation to drive value creation in the public sector. In the Appendix, we have outlined the calculations and related details of the Public Service Value methodology.

The Public Service Value Model is not intended to be a backdoor means of evaluating public performance and managers. This is not an audit of an organization or its managers. What's past is past. A key benefit of using the Public Service Value approach is the ability to ask, "Based on these performance patterns, what will be the outcome of our spending and managerial choices in the future?"

There is more work to do to further define the concept of public value, particularly in finding ways to identify, recognize and reconcile what can sometimes be competing or even conflicting views of citizens, taxpayers, service recipients and politicians. We plan to contribute to that in further research and study. In the meantime, we offer the Public Service Value methodology as a set of tools and techniques to help public service managers link action to outcome as they plot their journey to high performance.

Note on Sources

Unless otherwise noted, all direct quotations are from interviews conducted by members of Accenture's global Public Service Value team with public sector performance measurement experts and government practitioners

Acknowledgements

The authors would like to thank the many people who contributed to this book through interviews, assessments of the Public Service Value Model, and reviews of the manuscript.

In particular, we would like to thank the following people for sharing their time and insights: Adalsteinn Brown, Information Management Lead for the Health Results Team, Ontario Ministry of Health and Long Term Care; Mark Catlett, former CFO, U.S. Department of Veterans Affairs; John Eckhart, Director of the Indiana Department of Revenue; Elliot Hibbs, retired Director of the Arizona Department of Revenue; Ken Miller, retired Director of the Indiana Department of Revenue; Lowell Richards, Director, Port Planning and Development, Massport; Ian Watmore, Head of the Prime Minister's Delivery Unit, United Kingdom; Chris Yapp, Head of Public Sector Innovation, Microsoft; Gene Leganza, Forrester Research; Dave McClure, Gartner; Brian Riedl, Heritage Foundation; Alan Webber, Forrester Research; Nicholas Barr, London School of Economics; Patrick Dunleavy, London School of Economics; Scott Fritzen, Lee Kuan Yew School of Public Policy, National University of Singapore; George Gettinby, Strathclyde University; Steve Kelman and Mark Moore, John F. Kennedy School of Government, Harvard University; Kenneth Matwiczak, Lyndon B. Johnson School of Public Affairs at the University of Texas, Austin; Maurice McTigue, Mercatus Institute at George Mason University; and Dennis Smith, Robert F. Wagner Graduate School of Public Service, New York University.

We would also like to thank our xixeditorial team for their advice and tireless help in preparing this book for publication: Vivienne Jupp, Laura Kopec, Scott McMurray, Lisa Neuberger, Philip von Haehling and Mark Younger.

Thanks to all of our Accenture colleagues who helped us over the past three years with the development of the Public Service Value Model and with the creation of this book.

Chapter 1

The Public Sector Squeeze

As public managers around the world seek ways to do more with less, the need is growing for a practical approach to define, measure and drive high performance in the public sector. Although public managers' budgets remain tight, taxpayers demand more, and better, service from public service organizations. Particularly in times of crisis, taxpayers question the value their governments are delivering to them. The increasing use of the Internet has further raised the bar on the level of service expected by the public. Some governments employ selective contracting out and privatization to raise productivity.

Elliott Hibbs must have felt as if he were caught in the jaws of a giant vise. During the first few months of 2003, the State of Arizona's newly appointed Director of the Department of Revenue found his agency had taken severe budget cuts for several years due to a state-wide austerity plan, in spite of its role as the major revenue producer for the State. Meanwhile, stakeholders ranging from legislators to taxpayers were demanding continued high levels of processing, enforcement and taxpayer assistance services without adequate resources to deliver those services. In addition, the prior administration had taken resources from enforcement and moved them to the service delivery side of the agency to meet the demands for swift refund processing, adversely impacting the effectiveness of the department, particularly in collecting unpaid taxes. As part of the new administration and to combat what appeared to be a serious decline in agency function and capabilities, Hibbs presented a plan to the legislature to restore department resources to 2002 levels by improving processing while increasing aggressive collection of delinquent taxes.

Hibbs, an Arizona state government veteran of more than 20 years, was confident that the initial steps he took at the agency were improving the agency's performance and adding value for many stakeholders. He reassigned staff back to audit and enforcement activities and continued a major upgrade of the agency's computer systems, which had started prior to his arrival. Yet he was frustrated with the lack of good data and meaningful facts that could help sell his message to the legislature, that cutting the Revenue Department's budget was a short-sighted fiscal act. "We were accomplishing a lot in spite of getting budget reductions or not enough increases to even cover higher personnel and operations costs. We couldn't easily get the legislature to see the importance of the value we were adding for the people of Arizona," he said. Caught in this dilemma, Hibbs agreed to pilot the Public Service Value methodology as a way of allocating resources to areas that would create the most value for Arizona taxpayers. Along with other public managers around the world at that time, Hibbs was facing a public sector squeeze. He needed to find a way to create value with scarce resources.

Public Service Value Approach

Like Director Hibbs, readers wrestling with the challenges of delivering value in the public sector may find Figure 1.1 helpful. It can be used to frame discussions with public managers about choices and trade-offs available to increase outcomes, or end results of programs, as cost-effectively as possible. The Public Service Value Model is a framework that public managers can use to set priorities between several goals and objectives. By our definition, high-performance governments are those that increase public value—they are able to efficiently produce more or improved outcomes for the public monies spent.

The Public Service Value approach has been developed over the past few years with the help of dozens of government organizations and academic experts. Using the Public Service Value Model, a public manager can evaluate an organization's ability to achieve key social outcomes cost-effectively and aggregate these results to provide an indicative measure of relative public value creation.

Public service organizations can plot their performance on the Public Service Value Model diagram (see Figure 1.1). The direction

FIGURE 1.1

The Public Service Value Model

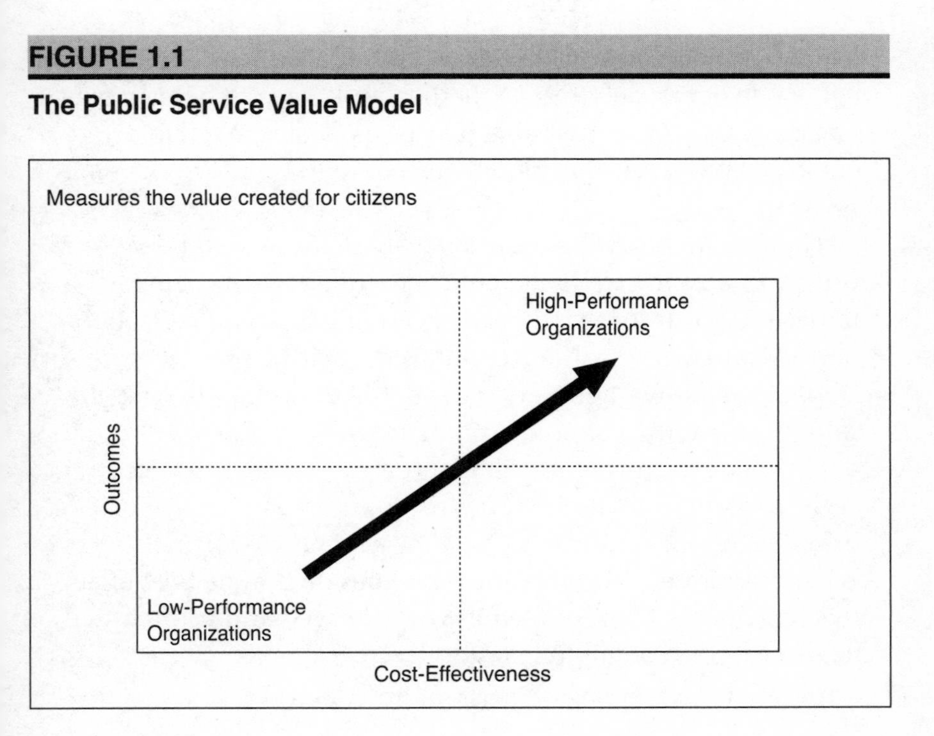

that an organization moves from year to year reveals how performance is trending. For example, if an organization moves to the upper right-hand quadrant, it is succeeding in increasing outcomes and cost-effectiveness at the same time. On the other hand, if a public service organization increases outcomes but is not cost-effective, it will move toward the upper left-hand quadrant. An organization that manages its costs, but sees a reduction in outcomes, will move toward the lower right-hand quadrant. In these last two cases, when done deliberately, organizations are making explicit trade-offs between focusing on improved outcomes and increasing cost-efficiency in order to, in effect, maintain public value. Lastly, if an organization heads into the lower left-hand

Value Turnaround

In 2003, Hibbs applied the Public Service Value Model to his agency to better determine whether, and how, his agency was adding value on a cost-effective basis. Using available revenue agency data, the model uncovered some eye-opening results.

The Public Service Value analysis demonstrated that the previous administration's policy of over-emphasizing customer service at the expense of tax compliance and collections had destroyed value compared with the Revenue Department's average performance. The model also graphically illustrated, using directional arrows to track annual department performance, that the steps taken beginning in early 2003 were creating value (see Figure 1.2).

While it still had a long way to go, the Department was achieving more of its strategic outcomes on a more cost-effective basis. How those outcomes were derived and tracked will be discussed in detail in Chapter Four.

FIGURE 1.2

Arizona Department of Revenue Public Service Value Performance Matrix

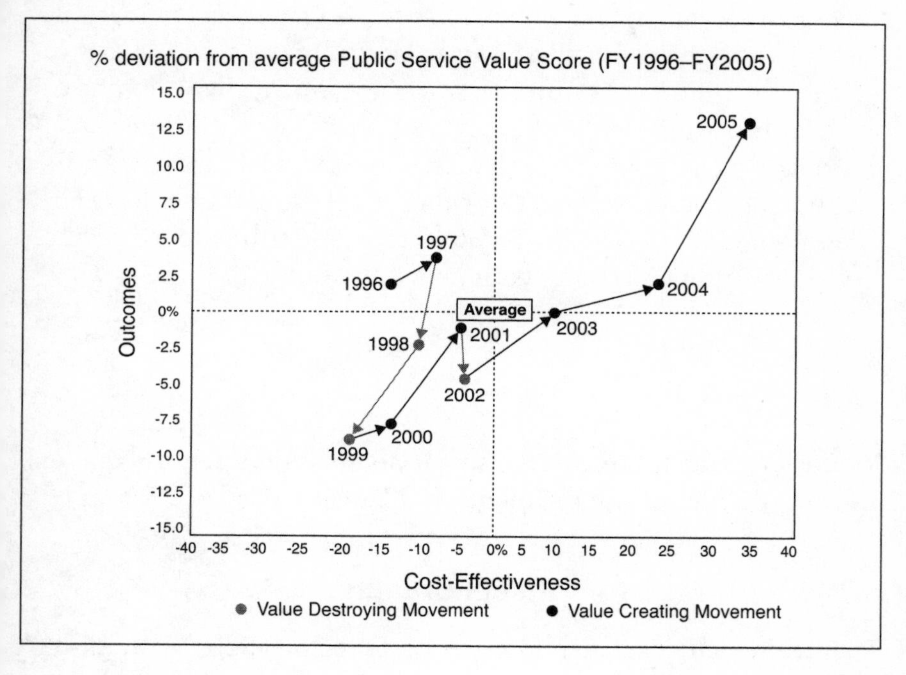

quadrant, it is experiencing a reduction of both outcomes and cost-effectiveness and is eroding public value and most likely taxpayers' confidence.

The Public Service Value approach to helping public managers define and increase value in the public sector was inspired by the principles of Shareholder Value Analysis, which is commonly used to understand the performance of companies. In the private sector, a company's shareholder generally sees the value of his or her investment increase with company earnings, which are ultimately reflected in the company's share price. For the Public Service Value

Public Service

Our definition of public service is meant to be inclusive to encompass all organizations that are engaged in delivering services to the public that are, at least in part, paid for using taxpayer money. Public service organizations therefore include government agencies, nonprofit organizations and private sector companies that provide services that have traditionally been delivered primarily by governments. The determination of what is a public service is ultimately a political determination by governments.

Model, we substitute private sector shareholders with taxpayers, citizens, public service recipients and legislators.

Fiscal Crunch

The "value squeeze" experienced by Director Hibbs is an all-too-familiar challenge shared by public managers worldwide (see Figure 1.3). In the United Kingdom, for example, Ian Watmore, who in 2004 was appointed to the newly created position of Chief Information Officer and is now the head of the Prime Minister's Delivery Unit, said, "It is difficult to balance the objectives of delivering social outcomes and services that consume more resources in an era when governments have less to spend on this rising demand." Since public managers are continually asked to do more with less, the questions on everyone's mind are:

- How does one determine if taxpayer money spent is actually improving government performance?
- How does one tell if public service programs are adding value?

FIGURE 1.3

The Public Sector Squeeze

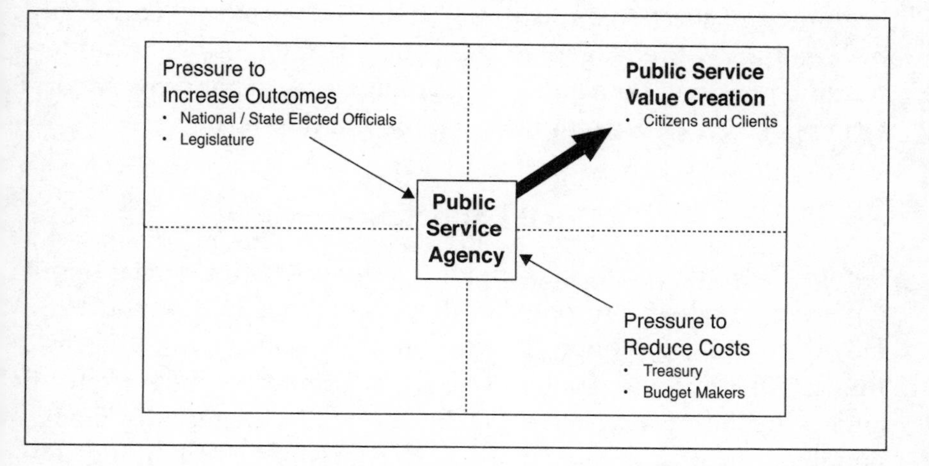

Politicians, like public managers, feel the squeeze when it comes to delivering value. Politicians feel pressure to deliver on voters' expectations for education, security, social services, pensions and health care. The pressure on budgets in most countries is unlikely to lessen significantly in the years ahead. One significant factor driving this fiscal crunch in most of Europe (particularly in France and Germany), Japan and the United States is the rapid aging of the population and the demands that population is putting on the social security and health care systems in these countries.

In the United States, for example, spending on Social Security, Medicare and Medicaid total roughly 8 percent of the gross domestic product (GDP). By 2030, according to the Congressional Budget Office, the cost of these programs is projected to consume about 15 percent of GDP, and by 2050 they could equal about 19 percent of GDP.[1] Brian Riedl, a budget analyst with the Heritage Foundation, noted, "The coming entitlement crunch is looking increasingly dire."

The budget outlook at the state and municipal level in the

United States is not more encouraging. States continue to shoulder heavy Medicaid-related health care costs. With few exceptions, many states also were unprepared for the fiscal downturn at the beginning of the new millennium. Some either borrowed heavily by issuing debt, engaged in budgetary maneuvering by underfunding pension or other long-term obligations to help cover short-term operating deficits, or both, to ride out the storm.

Great Expectations

It might seem logical for stakeholders to reduce their expectations of government when confronted with such obvious budget squeezes. However, quite the opposite reaction often seems to be the case. Interest in improving public sector performance comes from all angles, including taxpayers, public service recipients, the media, nongovernmental organizations and legislators. If anything, the prospect of a perennial budget crunch serves to increase calls from all stakeholders for a more efficient return on taxpayers' money. Public managers, already interested in finding new and improved ways to deliver public services, are reaffirmed in their efforts.

In 2004, twelve years after co-authoring the influential *Reinventing Government*, David Osborne published another important contribution to the debate on public value, *The Price of Government*, with co-author Peter Hutchinson. Osborne and Hutchinson have tracked spending at the federal level, as well as at state and local levels, in the United States for the past several decades. They demonstrated that since the early 1970s federal revenues (all taxes, fees and charges), as a percentage of aggregate personal income, trended within a fairly narrow range, averaging slightly more than 20 percent. At the state and local levels, the cost of government during this same period stayed within even narrower ranges of 7 to 8 percent for state, and 6 percent for local.[2]

Osborne and Hutchinson's findings suggest that, at least intuitively, Americans in the post–World War II era have had a fairly consistent sense of an acceptable range of what they are prepared to pay for public services. If taxes trend too low, citizens complain about inadequate services and social inequities. If they trend too high, taxpayers and politicians start pounding the table for tax cuts.

The authors note that despite almost three decades of conservative politicians in the United States and elsewhere singing the praises of smaller government from the early 1970s to the late 1990s, "Citizens do not just want lower taxes and 'cheap government.' In reality, they constantly demand more from government, but at a relatively fixed price. They are in effect pressing for more value each year for the money they pay. In this respect, government is challenged by the same forces that constrain any other provider of goods and services."[3]

Acknowledging the projected spiraling health care and Social Security entitlement costs of the next few decades, Osborne and Hutchinson do not speculate as to whether, or to what extent, such pressures could force the "price" of government to ratchet sharply higher and become stable at an elevated plateau. They only point out that the sole precedent for such a dramatic repricing of government in the United States was triggered by a world war hard on the heels of a global depression. It occurred in the 1940s when federal taxes increased dramatically to pay for World War II. Once the U.S. economy had stabilized by the early 1950s, the price of government (which included significantly greater benefits and services than before the Depression) remained fairly constant, albeit significantly higher than prewar levels, for the next 50 years.[4]

Generally, governments do not follow a budget process that takes into account the price of government as described by Osborne and Hutchinson. Deal making at the eleventh hour typically results in a compromise budget, although as Osborne and Hutchinson point out, such deals do not always share voters' priorities or recognize that taxpayers in effect put limits on what they are willing to pay.

The Right Questions

In the wake of a fiscal crisis or natural disaster, citizens tend to hold their governments more accountable for delivering value than when politics as usual and competing special interests alone frame such discussions. As Mark Catlett, a former chief financial officer for the Department of Veterans' Affairs, noted, "Whenever there is a major catastrophe, people ask the right questions." Of course, the challenge for public managers and stakeholders is to find a means of asking the "right questions" about public value absent a crisis.

Nonetheless, national crises, whether terrorist attacks, severe economic downturns or natural disasters, do tend, at least temporarily, to throw the "price of government" off-kilter as spending spikes to help offset the impact of the crisis. The aftermath of a crisis is one of the periods during which citizen and legislative stakeholders stand back and reappraise the value they are receiving from public service organizations. Under such circumstances, stakeholders are more likely to look at how public service organizations performed, or failed to perform, in response to the crisis. A case in point is Hurricane Katrina, which devastated portions of the Gulf Coast of the United States, including New Orleans, in August 2005.

A good deal of public debate following the hurricane centered on the federal funding of levee maintenance and improvements in New Orleans. Questions were raised. If more money had been spent on the levee construction to make them able to withstand a more severe hurricane like Katrina, rather than a lesser storm as constructed, there may have been a different outcome. The consequences of resource allocation decisions are brought home to stakeholders at such times.

Another good example of how public value concepts can guide government decision-making is well illustrated by the U.K. government response to two major national crises concerning cattle over the past 20 years.

First, in the late 1980s, British cattle started to develop a degenerative brain disease. Bovine spongiform encephalopathy (BSE) is a chronic disorder affecting the central nervous system of cattle, popularly known as mad cow disease. When it first appeared, the government's response, in light of the scientific knowledge available at the time, was one of public reassurance and playing down the magnitude of the problem. However, over several years, more cattle became infected and serious questions were asked about the possible transmission of BSE to humans. When in 1996 a potential link was made between a new variant of Creutzfeldt-Jakob disease in humans and BSE, the government had to take drastic action. A series of protective measures was introduced, including the purchase for destruction of cattle more than 30 months of age (which were believed to carry the greatest risk for BSE infection). The European Union imposed a ban on the export of beef from the United Kingdom, and the United Kingdom banned certain cuts of beef, such as T-bone steaks, from domestic consumption because they contained vertebral column, which was potentially infected.

The costs of the slaughter program and other measures ran into the hundreds of millions of pounds, and the effect on the British cattle industry was devastating. BSE eventually subsided and no epidemic of Creutzfeldt-Jakob disease has yet materialized. To date, there have been fewer than 200 cases. Many of the measures introduced by the United Kingdom have been included in the BSE eradication and prevention programs instituted by the European Union and other countries where BSE has occurred. The effectiveness of these controls can be seen in the rapid decline in the number of cases.

However, the BSE episode diminished public value. Public health outcomes declined as the public's confidence in food safety was eroded and the British beef industry was badly damaged. While the outcome of containing BSE was eventually achieved, with the benefit of hindsight, not all of the measures taken were either necessary or successful and some of the money spent had little or no effect on the outcome. However, beef consumption has been restored to previous levels and the beef industry is recovering.[5]

Then in early 2001, the U.K. government had to deal with a second major livestock crisis. Foot and mouth disease (FMD) was discovered in a herd of pigs in the north of England. FMD is an infectious disease affecting cloven-hoofed animals, in particular cattle, sheep, pigs, goats and deer. The disease is serious for animal health and for the economics of the livestock industry. While FMD is not normally fatal to adult animals, it is debilitating and causes significant loss of productivity. For example, milk yields may drop or the animals may become lame. In young animals it can be fatal.

Given the recent experience of BSE, the U.K. government response focused on four key outcomes:

1. Rapid reassurance to the public that the problem was being addressed
2. Limiting the impact on the British farming industry
3. Containing the cost
4. Bringing the disease under control

Usual practice with FMD is to slaughter the immediately infected stock, to slaughter stock known to have had contact with infected stock, to limit the movement of stock and to control all access to infected areas. Vaccination of animals that might be exposed to infection is now recommended as the final measure to limit the spread of the disease. However, having vaccinated animals would limit the ability of the European Union and United Kingdom to trade freely on the world market. In addition, this would have yet again brought into question the quality of British livestock, which had only recently begun to be reestablished after BSE.

The U.K. government, conscious of the outcome of minimizing impact on the farming industry, decided against vaccination for a multitude of reasons. Instead, it implemented a policy of culling all animals within a given geographic range of a known outbreak, whether they were known to have had contact or not. This policy led to the cull of over 4.2 million animals before the outbreak was contained.[6]

On this occasion, focus on two particular outcomes—the need to contain the spread of the disease without risking the status of the herd by using vaccination—proved to be expensive while, given the high-level of media attention, still not effectively providing reassurance that the disease was being effectively managed. Public value was again called into question as commentators in the press and Parliament asked whether the cost of the measures taken was proportionate to the outcomes delivered. E.U. and U.K. government guidelines for managing future outbreaks of FMD have now been changed to put a greater emphasis on vaccination.[7]

As both examples illustrate, natural disasters present a number of public value challenges:

- Governments must react quickly, often with less than complete information.
- The desired outcomes could be unclear and might well conflict.
- It is easy to spend money ineffectually where the desired outcomes have not been established as government seeks to respond rapidly to an emerging crisis.

In this context, a Public Service Value analysis could bring new rigor to contingency planning for natural disasters. Conducting such an analysis could help public managers think through, in a structured manner and without the pressure attending an actual crisis, what the desired outcomes would be in response to a given disaster. A Public Service Value analysis would help public officials examine the trade-offs that they would need to consider when dealing with such an emergency. In addition, Public Service Value analysis can be used to evaluate responses to disasters so that future disaster planning can be improved.

The Public Performance Gap

There is increased pressure on public service organizations to open additional channels of communication for servicing and informing the public. One early initiative that New York City Mayor Michael

Bloomberg took on when elected in 2001 was to improve the level of service that city agencies provided New Yorkers. For example, simply listing phone numbers for the sprawling city government, which provided more than 900 different services through more than 50 agencies, consumed 14 pages of the New York City phone book. The Bloomberg Administration wanted a single contact number, with live operators handling callers' queries, to improve government responsiveness. The operators would access a constantly updated knowledge base to quickly provide directory assistance, information or services to citizens, businesses and visitors. In 2003 the city launched its widely acclaimed "311" service, providing a simple number to call for all nonemergency services and information. The program, which has recently been handling over 40,000 calls a day and received over 240,000 calls on the first day of the December 2005 transit strike, has increased government responsiveness and citizen satisfaction while at the same time significantly reducing the city's call center costs.

The pressure exerted on public sector performance is happening around the world from the citizens of Indiana (who want electronic service from the Indiana Department of Revenue to match what they receive from the private sector), to the people of Spain (who are pressing for greater access to information about retirement and other benefits from their Instituto Nacional de la Seguridad Social [INSS]). At the INSS, public managers have answered this demand through technological modernization and a citizen-based approach. Among the measures adopted by the agency is a new web site that offers citizens electronic access to administrative forms and other information, as well as new in-person citizen centers and a toll-free telephone information system.

Indeed, a multicountry report published in 2005 by Accenture, "Leadership in Customer Service: New Expectations, New Experiences," concluded that among the 22 nations surveyed, "Citizens' willingness to embrace a new generation of services outpaces governments' ability to deliver them."[8] Canada, which ranked number one in three of the four facets of leadership in customer service measured by the study, endeavors to provide superior citizen service. The Canadian government's experience with its Government On-Line program has led the country to the recognition that taking the next step to service transformation implies a radical change in the way government as a whole is managed. As a result, Canada has recently articulated a service vision to redesign services, service delivery and public service itself to achieve dramatic improvements in client satisfaction, cost savings and efficiencies, policy outcomes and accountability and transparency. The vision specifies achievement of outcomes within a framework defined by citizens' needs and a whole-of-government approach to service delivery.[9]

If anything, the pressure on public service organizations to create more technology-driven service options, driven largely by citizens' increased use of the Internet, is only likely to expand in the coming years. Alan Webber, an analyst with Forrester Research, and formerly an analyst with the U.S. Department of the Interior, has observed "As technology pushes us forward and networking on the Internet or elsewhere becomes more ubiquitous, people are looking for government to perform the same way. Or at least they want it to trend a lot more in that direction."

Fostering Competition in Government

In the private sector, competition for customers and capital typically forces performance improvements. High-performance businesses offering innovative products or services tend to attract new customers and outperform industry laggards, expanding and adding employees in the process. Also, they attract capital as investors bid up their share price, or purchase newly issued shares, in anticipation that the company's high growth rate will produce a high return on investors' capital. Competitors are forced to improve their performance or risk withering away or being acquired by another market player. Investors tend to pull their money out of such companies by selling their shares and buying shares of higher-performing businesses.

However, in the public sector, competition has played a less direct role in improving performance. Until recently, the closest thing to competition in the public sector was competition among political parties or officials for votes. A newly elected candidate could declare a citizen mandate and bring in new governing policies. However, a new and growing form of competition in government is the contracting out of certain services. In select cases, where government used to be the sole provider, some nations, states and municipalities have decided to contract services out to be more efficient. Refuse collection is a common example, in many countries, of the private sector performing a tax-supported public sector job relatively efficiently. In the United States, for example, private companies today manage about 70 percent of the waste generated by local municipalities.[10] Private sector haulers typically bid against each other for a municipality's multiyear garbage hauling contract. While there have been some scandals in the garbage collection industry, the private sector competition generally has proved to be an efficient means to raise the large amounts of capital needed to fund the purchase of fleets of garbage trucks and other equipment. A key part of the price haulers charge the city is determined by how efficiently they can raise capital in the private markets to fund purchases of trucks and other capital equipment. The hauler proposing the most efficient and effective economic model usually wins the contract, helping to boost the cost-efficiency and possibly service levels of local governments and thus helping make taxpayers' money go farther.

Privatization and the contracting out of public services have tested the degree to which private sector competition in the public sector can help improve government performance. Privatization (where a service previously provided by the government moves into the private sector) and contracting out (where services are provided by a private sector company, but still paid for by government) has been gaining ground at all levels of government for at least the past two decades. These practices have been especially widespread in New Zealand, the United States and the United Kingdom, and the moves to introduce competition into public services have provided added impetus to the trend toward fostering high performance in the rest of the public sphere.

New Zealand Success

Nationalization of major industries in New Zealand in the wake of World War II followed a path similar to that set by post-war government in the United Kingdom. And like the United Kingdom, New Zealand by the late 1970s and early 1980s was eyeing privatization as a means of improving economic efficiency, creating more jobs and, in essence, adding public value.[11] Beginning in the mid-1980s, New Zealand started the task of privatizing many of its state-owned industries, including railroads, rural banks, telecommunications and public works. "They had become a vehicle for soaking up unemployment, they were massively overstaffed," said Maurice McTigue, a former New Zealand cabinet officer who led much of the privatization, and who currently serves as director of the Government Accountability Project at the Mercatus Center, George Mason University. To ease the pain of layoffs, the national government took significant up-front buy-out costs, noted McTigue, although the scope of the layoffs did trigger initial public resentment. In the railroad sector, for instance, employment plunged from 28,000 to 5,000, while in the telecom sector payrolls were slashed by 50 percent. The government operated the enterprises as profit-making companies for a few years, and converted them to full accrual-based accounting, before offering shares in the companies to the public.

Public opinion reversed itself within a few years as sharp improvements in public services and efficiency drove customer satisfaction, and it became clear that privatization was adding public value. The waiting time for a new phone line, for example, fell from around 6 weeks to just 24 hours in most of the country. The cost of residential and business service fell by 58 percent and 69 percent, respectively, in just three years. Competition in the telecom sector increased to such an extent following deregulation that within three years total employment actually exceeded preprivatization levels by 30 percent. In the railroad sector, shipping rates fell by 55 percent, and the railroads by the late 1980s were posting annual profits for the first time in three decades.

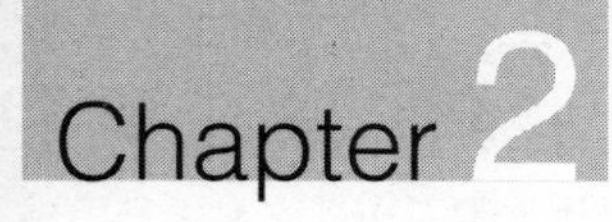

Chapter 2

Zeroing In on Outcomes

The importance of focusing on outcomes has been recognized by public service organizations around the world as they attempt to bolster their ability to measure, manage and improve performance. Over the past two decades, we have observed a growing trend in many countries to pass legislation and put forth national mandates for government organizations to use performance management and, in some cases, to focus more on outcomes. Academic literature from this same period gives public service organizations some guidance on outcome management.

Alan Webber, who joined Forrester Research as a senior analyst after leaving government, was not surprised by a conversation about "e-government" initiatives he had with an official at the U.S. Office of Management and Budget (OMB) in the summer of 2005. The OMB official told Webber that his agency was "finally really focusing on the citizen." Webber said he asked the OMB official, what had he been focusing on before? The official was briefly flustered, then said, "We've always been focused on the citizen, we're just finally figuring out how to measure how well we're doing the job for the citizen."

Finally figuring out "how well we're doing the job." In other words, the official was acknowledging, the OMB was beginning to focus on outcomes. Like the OMB, public service organizations around the world are increasingly focusing on outcomes. Yet, even in countries where there are national mandates requiring outcome measurement, experience has shown that there are many barriers to adoption that can delay or derail efforts.

Outputs versus Outcomes

As noted in Figure 2.1, there is a wide spectrum of measures ranging from inputs to outcomes. *Inputs* represent the resources of various types—financial, workforce and so forth—invested in delivering a service. *Processes* are a series of actions or operations conducted to achieve a goal. *Outputs* are the products, goods or services delivered. *Outcomes* are the impacts, benefits or consequences for the public that those goods and services are designed to attain.

Theodore Poister contrasts outputs and outcomes in *Measuring Performance in Public and Nonprofit Organizations*, explaining, "Outputs represent what a program actually does, whereas outcomes are the results it produces."[1] An outcome is an end result experienced by the citizen, but it is often confused with outputs, which are the specific products or services delivered. For instance, increasing passenger safety is an outcome desired by public transportation agencies and society. Although the output of increasing the number of security officers is a means to achieve this outcome, it is meaningless in itself if we cannot relate it to an outcome that the public actually wants and needs, such as reduced incidents of theft.

In addition, outcomes have a time element and can be short-term, intermediate-term, or long-term. The long-term or end outcomes, such as increasing community safety or reducing the incidence of a disease, take the most time to materialize and can be difficult to measure. In this book, we do not distinguish between short-term, intermediate-term, and long-term outcomes. However, if we did, we would find that many of the outcomes we reference are in the short-term or intermediate-term category, since we are focusing on particular organizations and ways to help improve their specific performance. An interesting additional aspect of this is that a focus on long-term outcomes would probably need to account for a group of organizations or an entire sector to be able to encompass all of the factors that contribute to achieving an end outcome.

Clarity on Outcomes

If public managers have a clear understanding of an organization's outcomes, they are better equipped to find ways to deliver those outcomes to the public.

Outcomes often loom large in the public debate when a new public service is being established or an existing one expanded, such as building new hospitals, or creating an after-school program

FIGURE 2.1

Inputs, Processes and Outputs versus Outcomes

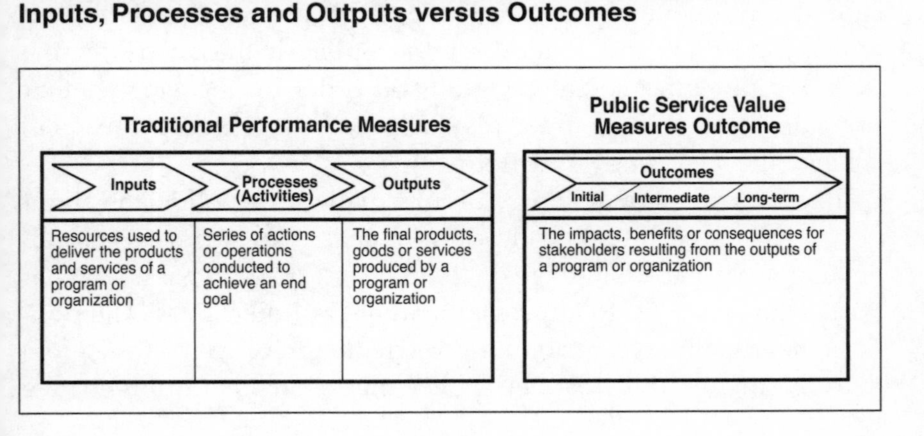

in the inner city. Indeed, when the modern welfare states were created in many Western countries in the mid-twentieth century, it seemed that there was a clear view of what the outcomes should be.

For example, in the United Kingdom, Sir William Beveridge in his 1942 report recommended that government find ways to fight the five "giant evils" of want, disease, ignorance, squalor and idleness. His report led to a fundamental rethinking of how to provide services such as public health, education and housing. More than 60 years later, Sir William would probably not be able to find his five "giant evils" in England, where the quality of public health, housing and the general standard of living has been immeasurably improved. Many of the "evils" of the early twentieth century have been largely tackled, in the developed world at least, by vaccination, public hygiene, improved nutrition, wider education and better housing. But, what should be done about those of the early twenty-first century? For example, Alzheimer's disease, the consequences of obesity and the spread of viral illnesses in an age of rapid global transportation all require new approaches in the fight against "disease." While eradicating disease remains as important an outcome now as it was during Beveridge's time, how that outcome can be achieved today has changed considerably.

Some governments at the national, state or local level regularly conduct performance audits of government, including special commissions designed specifically to evaluate whether programs should continue to be funded. These efforts are commendable and will generate the most value for the public if they consider the intended outcomes of the programs in order to uncover whether priorities have shifted and if they help find more efficient ways to achieve the same or even better results.

Elections are a great source of information for politicians about how public expectations and priorities change over time. The public may not use the language of "outcomes," but voters know what they want and need to improve the quality of their lives. The public is more likely to care about how safe their city seems (outcome) than the mere number of new police on the streets (inputs) or the number of speeding tickets given (outputs). If politicians are to continue to connect with their constituents, they must become fluent in the language of outcomes.

In November 2005, the voters of the State of Washington gave the State Auditor's Office a unique charge—they said the office should do performance audits for *all* units of government in the state (state agencies, local governments, K-12 school districts, higher education institutions and special districts), and, most importantly, they designated a stream of revenue (a small, but significant, portion of sales tax receipts) to fund the audits. Another key part of the voter-approved ballot initiative is that audited organizations *must* implement the auditors' recommendations, or explain publicly why they will not do so. This initiative puts the Washington State Auditor's Office in a unique position to very strongly influence change throughout all of government in the State.

Recognizing the significant opportunity before them, State Auditor Brian Sonntag and his Director of Performance Audits, Linda Long, decided to develop a strategic plan that would outline to the public and to the various government agencies in the state (who are understandably curious), just what they plan to accomplish with this newfound authority. At present, the plan is still in draft form, but includes some forward-looking components worth discussion:

> The vision statement says "By *continuously evaluating performance*, Washington governments will deliver results citizens' value" (emphasis added). This focus on continuous performance evaluation is probably unique in the auditing profession.
>
> The mission statement includes performance of thorough, professional, high-quality audits. But it also says the

Auditor's office will ". . . bring about improvements in government and its use of resources by facilitating a change from expenditure based to performance based management and reporting. . . ." The office is actually taking on the role of encouraging governments to focus more on performance, not just on expenditures.

One of the key outcomes the Auditor's office wants to achieve is "Washington governments are embracing performance management." Strategies the State will implement to achieve that outcome include: establishing a performance management best practice repository that Washington agencies can use; offering technical assistance to governments looking to move to performance management; and establishing and promoting a government performance evaluation framework (very much like the Public Service Value Model) that Washington governments can use.

It is both exciting and promising that the Auditor's Office is taking this progressive view of the role they can play in making performance management something more than an annual report card that governments produce in the State of Washington. The State Auditor's Office will not be able to accomplish their ambitious goals alone. However, they are starting a long-term change process where a sharp focus on outcomes and value is central to the program. Ultimately, this approach should have a positive impact on the citizens of Washington.

Fluency in outcomes can be liberating in the public sector. As debate focuses on the delivery of outcomes that meet citizen expectations rather than on the operation of traditional public services, the necessity and indeed desirability of changes and innovation in service delivery becomes more clear. And it is only through such innovation that significant changes in the production of public value can be achieved.

Self-Imposed Pressure

An increasing amount of the pressure to increase performance and focus on outcomes is being driven by governments themselves, including public managers and legislators around the world. Since the early 1990s, countries including the United Kingdom to Canada, Japan, France, Singapore, Germany and the United States have started introducing new legislation and national mandates aimed at shifting the focus of public sector performance measurement and management to outcomes.

Public Service Agreements in the United Kingdom

Almost from the moment of taking office in 1997, Tony Blair's "New Labour" Government made performance measurement a cornerstone of its governing policies. The country benefits both from a recent resurgence of interest in management, coupled with a homegrown and nurtured large, vibrant public sector.

In 1998, the U.K. government published public service agreements (PSAs) with outcomes and specific targets for each central government department. The PSAs, based on a zero-based spending analysis of programs initiated earlier in the year, focus on each department's aims and objectives and spell out what progress the government expects to make using specific targets and time lines.[2]

Prime Minister Blair personally keeps the performance management heat on the public sector. He routinely meets with a Cabinet secretary to review key agency performance targets. Said Steve Kelman, Weatherhead professor of public management, John F. Kennedy School of Government, Harvard University, "The U.K. is where there is the most energy around the idea of public-sector performance improvement."

Canadian Innovation in Performance Management

The Canadian federal government has a track record in promoting and using performance management techniques. In the early 1990s, the Auditor General's office conducted a series of pioneering studies on well-performing public agencies. By 1996, Canada enacted the Planning, Reporting and Accountability Structure (PRAS) policy framework, which provided departments and agencies with a basis for planning and management, as well as served as a solid foundation for communicating performance information to parliamentarians. In 1999, the Canadian government launched the Results for Canadians campaign to encourage federal organizations to become more focused on taxpayers' needs and work in collaboration with other levels of government as well as the private and nonprofit sectors. Under one key portion of the campaign—Management, Resources and Results Structure (MRRS) policy—government agency activities and results are tracked in relationship to each other and to the overall outcomes to which they contribute. The MRRS policy went into effect April 1, 2005, replacing the old PRAS policy framework.

In November 2004, the Canadian national government received an award for excellence in reporting from the Canadian Institute of Chartered Accountants, acknowledging its leadership in adopting full accrual accounting in the 2003 Public Accounts of Canada, a full three years ahead of schedule. It joins Australia and New Zealand in having moved to full accrual accounting, which provides improved information for decision making and accountability, and a more comprehensive picture of government finances.

As part of a sweeping policy change that took effect April 1, 2005, the Canadian government adopted a Management Accountability Framework that "focuses on management results rather than required capabilities; provides a basis of engagement with departments; and suggests ways for departments both to move forward and to measure progress."[3] The government adds that "all government decisions must be framed by enduring public service values and the capacity to grow, learn, and innovate."[4]

The Government of Canada has grasped the importance of measuring performance but is still implementing the concept. Although many departments have adopted the concept wholeheartedly, however, there are others that still see it as more of a paper exercise. According to the Auditor General's reports, performance reports frequently fall short of criteria for good quality reporting. As a result, there is little evidence that performance measures are being used to make strategic decisions across all departments.

Shift to Define and Manage Outcomes Seen around the Globe

In 2004, Singapore's Ministry of Finance introduced its "Economy Drive." One of the main components of the campaign was its Net Economic Value Model (NEV). The goal of the model is to focus on performance management objectives. The amount of value created is measured by whether the organization or department has maximized outputs from a predetermined budget. If the success of NEV is defined by efficiently managing resources, then by all accounts NEV has been a success thus far. It is good at measuring how much it costs to do a specific activity but it does not capture whether or not a government organization is improving outcomes for its stakeholders as a result. To compensate for this, the Singapore government utilizes other mechanisms, such as the Balanced Scorecard, outcome statements and indicators, to measure program effectiveness.[5]

Singaporean culture is well suited to adopting a public value approach to improving government, noted Scott Fritzen, a professor at the Lee Kuan Yew School of Public Policy in Singapore. The country's political system is "a very technocratic system staffed with highly educated, highly capable people. They are orientated toward getting the maximum value they can from the bureaucracy."

Japan has also attempted to bring a focus on performance management in government. In June 2001, the Japanese government approved the Government Policy Evaluations Act (GPEA), which went into effect in April 2002. Through GPEA, the government hopes to require each administrative organization to conduct objective policy evaluations, reflect the results of these evaluations in the planning and development of policy and disseminate them to the public. Japan's introduction of GPEA has been successful in making the government more accountable. For example, within the Japanese Ministry of Internal Affairs and Communication, a goal of GPEA was to define its mission and strategy more clearly. Three years later, the organization has achieved this goal by clearly defining its mission and prioritizing its policies by selecting a subset of major policy areas and key metrics. One area where the Japanese government can further improve in its usage of GPEA is to establish strong linkages between GPEA results and the value levers involved in achieving a particular outcome. Success in creating these linkages will go a long way toward making GPEA a full-fledged strategic management tool.[6]

In August 2001, the French government created a framework for financial legislation (La Loi Organique Relative aux Lois de Finances, or LOLF) that crafted a five-year agenda for ministries to shift to a results-oriented form of management. Budgeting will shift from being based on categories of expenditure to "programmes" combining a coherent set of actions.[7] LOLF goes farther than most other countries' legislation in integrating outcome measurement with budgeting. By bringing the performance debate squarely into the budgeting process, LOLF goes a long way toward institutionalizing a national focus on outcomes and positively aligning the incentives of different stakeholders in the process.

Though home to the largest economy in continental Europe, Germany has lagged behind other countries in pursuing performance management objectives. After initial activities in the mid-1990s, Germany's "Modern State—Modern Administration" program has guided reform of the federal government since 1998. It focuses on three priorities: new public management, reducing bureaucracy and e-government. However, there is no explicit performance management legislation in Germany besides various experimentation clauses mainly in the budgeting and accounting context. The constitutional structure of the German government is one roadblock to the rapid adoption of performance measurement. The federal government has no authority to implement an integrated performance measurement framework without the support of the state and local governments.[8]

Legislating Accountability in the United States

In 1993, the Clinton administration shifted the debate in the United States about government performance with the National Performance Review (NPR), later renamed the National Partnership for

FIGURE 2.2

Recent National Performance Management Mandates

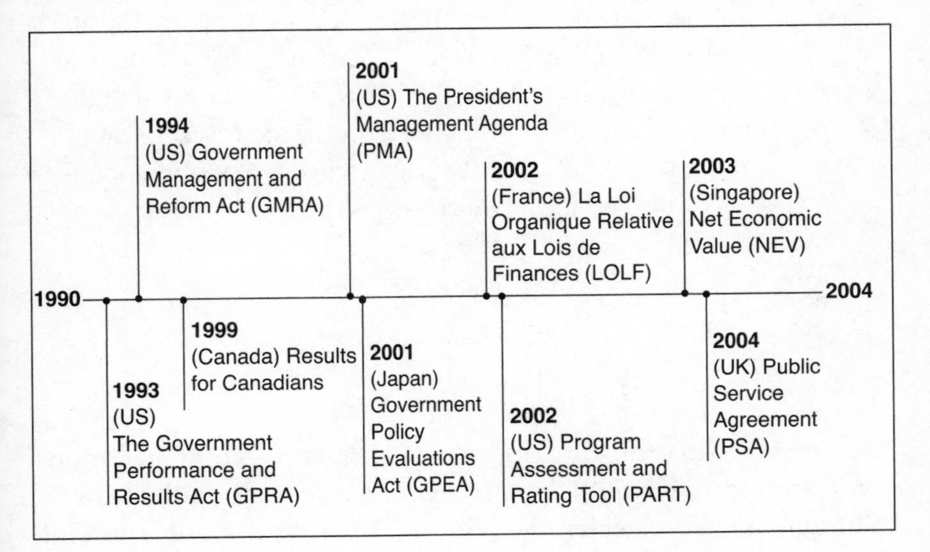

Technology Upgrades Spur Focus on Performance

During the 1990s, at the same time that the U.S. Government Performance and Results Act legislation was going into effect, U.S. federal government agencies as well as state and local governments were also upgrading their information technology (IT) systems. Advances in computing technologies, and the rapidly declining price for such systems, spurred the upgrades. The rush in the latter 1990s to upgrade IT systems in advance of the advent of the millennium, or "Y2K," as it became known, led to a stampede of technological upgrades. Indeed, the Y2K worries sparked one of the largest peacetime investments in technology by government and the private sector in history.

Once new IT systems were in place, public managers began to focus on getting their money's worth out of the new hardware and software. Indiana's Department of Revenue under former commissioner Ken Miller was an "early adopter" of the new technology. From the mid-1990s through 2004, Miller led a continued effort to keep the department advancing in public service offerings. The department had switched to a client-server IT system in the mid-1990s, ahead of most state departments in the United States, and a few years later became the first state revenue agency to use two-dimensional bar code reading of tax returns to capture documentation. That innovation enabled the department to reduce by half the number of people looking at returns, said Miller.

Reinventing Government. Consistent with the recommendations of the ground-breaking *Reinventing Government* manifesto of David Osborne and Ted Gaebler, the NPR initiative focused on applying entrepreneurial approaches used in the private sector to "reinvent" government processes in order to become more efficient and produce outcomes responsive to citizen needs.

The same year, President Clinton signed into law landmark legislation called the Government Performance and Results Act of 1993 (GPRA) that requires federal agencies to develop strategic plans with long-term, outcome-oriented goals and objectives, annual goals linked to achieving the long-term goals and annual reports on the results achieved. The rationale for driving GPRA through the U.S. Congress echoes the concerns that have led other governments to legislate performance management. The GPRA rationale included concerns that waste and inefficiency in federal programs were undermining public confidence in the U.S. government; that government managers would be better equipped to improve program efficiency if they focused more on articulating outcomes and had access to better performance information; and that congressional policymaking, spending decisions, and program oversight need to take into account program performance and results.

GPRA's focus on long-term goals and outcomes set it apart from earlier attempts at performance measurement. Starting in 1998, agencies' five-year strategic plans had to include comprehensive mission statements, specific goals and clear objectives. The OMB later added that agencies were required to update their strategic plans every three years. In addition, annual progress reports had to be submitted to describe the incremental progress the agency is making in achieving its longer-term goals.[9]

When President George W. Bush succeeded President Clinton in January 2001, the focus on public sector performance measurement continued unabated. Most recently, the President's Management Agenda (PMA), unveiled in 2001, and the Program Assessment and Rating Tool (PART), introduced the following year, supplement the goals set under GPRA.[10] The PMA measures federal agency performance in five areas: human capital, competitive sourcing, financial performance, e-government and budget/performance integration. On its web site, the OMB ranks federal agencies in terms of the five categories featured in the PMA, awarding a red, yellow or green light for performance in each category. This "executive branch management scorecard" may seem simplistic to some, yet it has the attention of federal bureaucrats. When federal bureaucrats focus on improving their PMA scorecard rankings, it is known as "getting to green."

Also developed and monitored by the OMB, PART is a diagnostic tool that is used to rate the effectiveness of federal programs with a particular focus on program results. The OMB's goal is to review all federal programs using PART over a five-year period, which began with a review of 20 percent of programs in fiscal 2004.

Turning Battleships

Despite the legislative mandate created by GPRA, outcome measurement is still not a mature practice in U.S. government departments and agencies. In its 10-year anniversary review of GPRA, submitted to Congress in March 2004, the General Accounting Office (GAO) concluded that "much work remains to be done" to make the U.S. federal government truly outcome oriented. Feedback from agency officials suggests that the performance measurement effort driven by GPRA remains too inwardly focused, looking at the processes of government, and not outwardly focused on the people government serves. Fewer than one in four of the federal agency officials interviewed by the GAO, which conducted the study, thought that GPRA had even a moderate impact on their ability to serve the public.[11]

Echoing the GAO's findings, Mark Catlett, a former chief financial officer of the Department of Veterans Affairs (VA), says that "we are turning this battleship," but not fast enough. Catlett does not think nearly enough progress is being made in focusing on outcomes at the federal government level, although agencies like the VA have done a good job of improving service delivery and access. He explains that "GPRA is first and foremost about performance measurement. It references outcomes, but they are not the focus."

According to Catlett, GPRA implementation does not get at the fundamental questions of government performance: Why are we funding that program? How do you know it makes a difference? PART starts to get at these underlying questions, he concedes, and for that reason it is treated by too many agencies as an external "OMB exercise," not something that drives internal annual management reviews. "While the VA has made significant progress, they are still in the measuring outputs mode," says Catlett. "How well they have improved in service delivery, the provision of health care and timeliness of payments—that's where the VA would like to focus." Across the board, basic performance measurement issues persist according to the GAO: "In some agencies, particularly those that have a research and development component, managers reported difficulties in establishing meaningful outcome measures."

Since Congress holds the purse strings, once it focuses on outcomes and makes spending decisions with outcomes in mind, agencies will have more incentive to focus on them also, according to Maurice McTigue, director of the Government Accountability Project at the Mercatus Center at George Mason University. "Congress does not appropriate funds based on outcomes," McTigue observes, "and until it does, federal administrators will not make true outcomes a priority." Agency officials also complained in the 2005 GAO report that, "Congress could make greater use of performance information to conduct oversight and to inform appropriations decisions. GPRA provides a vehicle for Congress to explicitly state its performance expectations in outcome-oriented terms when establishing new programs or in exercising oversight of existing programs that are not achieving desired results."[12]

An important challenge to getting legislatures to accept an outcome-oriented approach is the lack of trust or confidence that many legislators have in government agencies. Legislators are too often unwilling to accept at face value information they receive from agencies. They fear that agencies' concerns for self-preservation, if nothing else, are distorting the numbers they receive. For that reason, legislators tend to want to receive information on inputs and outputs they can independently verify, and only then move toward outcomes, either intuitively or with a conscious purpose. Many legislators believe that, as elected officials, it is their job to determine the social outcomes of public services.

In summary, although the goals of GPRA have yet to be fully achieved, its passage and implementation so far seem to have spawned a cascade of similar legislation across the United States, Canada, the United Kingdom, Japan, France, Singapore and other countries as nation after nation has hopped aboard the performance management bandwagon since the early 1990s.

Applying Private Sector Techniques

With government-initiated efforts to embrace outcome measurements mixed at best, public managers have increasingly tracked private sector management trends for ideas. The key problem has been to find management tools and techniques that do not rely primarily on contribution to profit as a primary incentive. Historically, the mix-and-match alternative—adding public service factors on to this private sector planning approach or on to that budgeting analysis, and using it to shock improved performance out of the public sector—has tended to end with predictably Frankenstein-like results.

Then came the Balanced Scorecard. It looked like it would meet the needs of the public service manager. Balanced Scorecard authors Kaplan and Norton, beginning with their 1992 article in the *Harvard Business Review* and followed by the 1996 publication of their book, *Balanced Scorecard*, critiqued the private sector's excessive focus on the bottom line. They argued that focusing on short-term financial results alone will not deliver long-term shareholder value. To do that, an organization also needs to focus on customers and on its own capabilities as well as on ensuring that it is engaged in the learning and development that will enable it to deliver value in the long term. The short-term bottom line does not equate to longer-term value delivery, as they reiterated in their 2000 book, *The Strategy-Focused Organization.*[13]

When the Balanced Scorecard was first published, it seemed that public managers finally could be freed from the tyranny of the private sector's short-term financial focus. Many rushed to embrace the new methodology. The importance that the Balanced Scorecard approach attached to focusing on operations and processes that lead to results (in addition to the finances that keep an organization afloat) was a welcome relief to many public managers. Since the ultimate goals of many public service programs may reside years in the future, focusing on measuring the intermediate-term steps that may contribute to achieving the long-term goals fits well with the way many public sector organizations operate. The Balanced Scorecard did not replace the need for a way to measure long-term value in the public sector, but it did provide public managers with a more-sophisticated tool to help them manage toward the organizations' long-term goals (see Figure 2.3).

"Rebalancing" the Scorecard for Government

The widespread adoption of some form of a Balanced Scorecard approach by thousands of public service organizations since its 1992 debut is a testament to the methodology's adaptability. The adoption in the private sector has been equally impressive, since nearly half of *Fortune* 1000 businesses have adopted a Balanced Scorecard approach. That success led the *Harvard Business Review* to include the Balanced Scorecard among the 75 most important ideas of the twentieth century.

Despite the eagerness of many public service organizations to use the Balanced Scorecard, it has been criticized by some public management scholars in the intervening years. A key criticism regarding its applicability to nonprofit organizations is that it still

FIGURE 2.3

The Balanced Scorecard

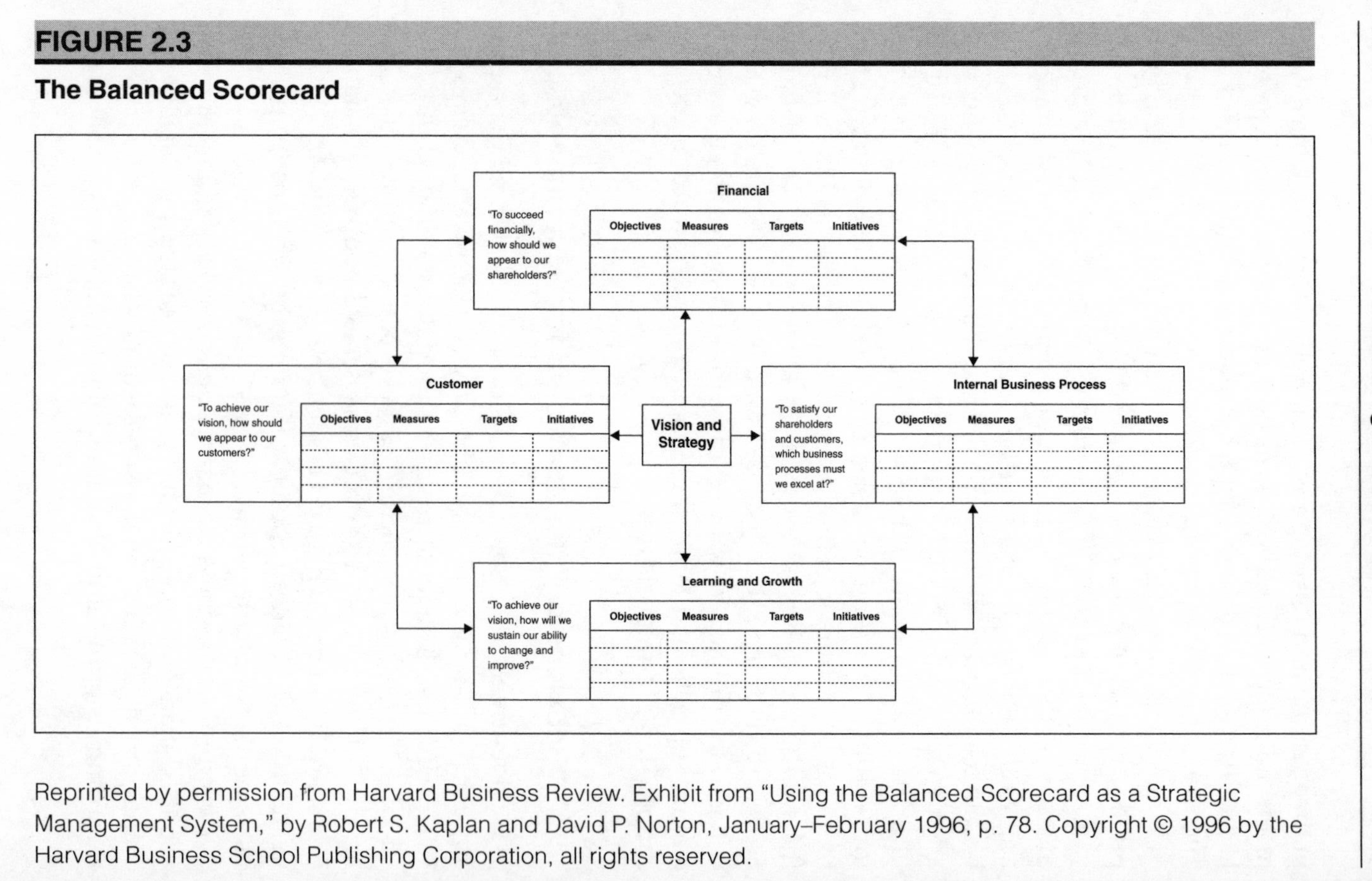

Reprinted by permission from Harvard Business Review. Exhibit from "Using the Balanced Scorecard as a Strategic Management System," by Robert S. Kaplan and David P. Norton, January–February 1996, p. 78. Copyright © 1996 by the Harvard Business School Publishing Corporation, all rights reserved.

puts too much emphasis on financial results. Mark Moore, director of the Hauser Center for Nonprofit Organizations at Harvard University's John F. Kennedy School of Government and a pioneering thinker about the concept of public value, observed in a May 2003 paper:

> The Balanced Scorecard recommended the use of non-financial measures not to change the goal from maximizing profits to something else, but *because financial measures alone could not help managers figure out how to sustain financial performance in the future.* In the non-profit sector, in contrast, what is important about non-financial measures is not that they help us to understand how to make more money, it is that the goals we seek to achieve through nonprofit organizations are social rather than financial, and that these accomplishments are best measured by non-financial measures.[14]

Moore also criticizes the Balanced Scorecard for embracing the private sector mantras of "competitive strategy" and "distinctive competence," which in many ways are not appropriate for the public sector. Instead, Moore argues that governments and nonprofit organizations should instead seek partnerships and cooperation with other players as a means of furthering their social goals:

> Because the goal of nonprofits is to achieve social results without worrying too much about earning financial or material rewards for doing so, it seems that nonprofit organizations should be willing to set aside their narrow interests in protecting their organization's competitive position for the broader purposes of achieving the desired results.[15]

Moore is correct in emphasizing the difference of social outcomes in nonprofits, but cost-effectiveness cannot be ignored by public service organizations. Outcomes are not "good" at any price, especially when governments around the world are struggling to do more with less. There has to be a financial dimension to measuring public value if only because the money that finances public value *is* public.

Strategy Maps: Getting There from Here

Navigating the long road to measuring public outcomes often requires, in addition to lots of persistence and dedication, a road map. Kaplan and Norton coined the phrase *strategy map*, and others use the term *logic model* almost interchangeably, to describe a graphic presentation for linking procedural steps and objectives with achieving strategic goals. As Kaplan and Norton described it in an article titled "Having Trouble with Your Strategy? Then Map It" in the September-October 2000 *Harvard Business Review*, "Strategy implies the movement of an organization from its present position to a desirable but uncertain future position. Because the organization has never been to this future place, the pathway to it consists of a series of linked hypotheses. A strategy map specifies these cause-and-effect relationships, which makes them explicit and testable."[16]

The reason to create a strategy map or logic model is to identify and clarify what goes into a program, what are the outputs in terms of products or services produced and what outcomes are supposed to be the end result. Such maps and models should by definition be tailored to define the specific steps followed by a particular program. That said, most strategy maps and logic models tend to follow a similar step-by-step process, so it is worthwhile to look at how a particular program relates to a fairly representative logic model, such as the one in Figure 2.4 from the United Way's teen mother parenting education program. The ultimate outcome in this example, babies achieving appropriate 12-month developmental milestones, follows from a series of intermediate-term outcomes focused on educating the teen mothers, which are the result of outputs tracking instruction and counseling that link all the way back to the inputs of staff, materials, facilities and funding.

FIGURE 2.4

Teen Mother Parenting Education Program Logic Model

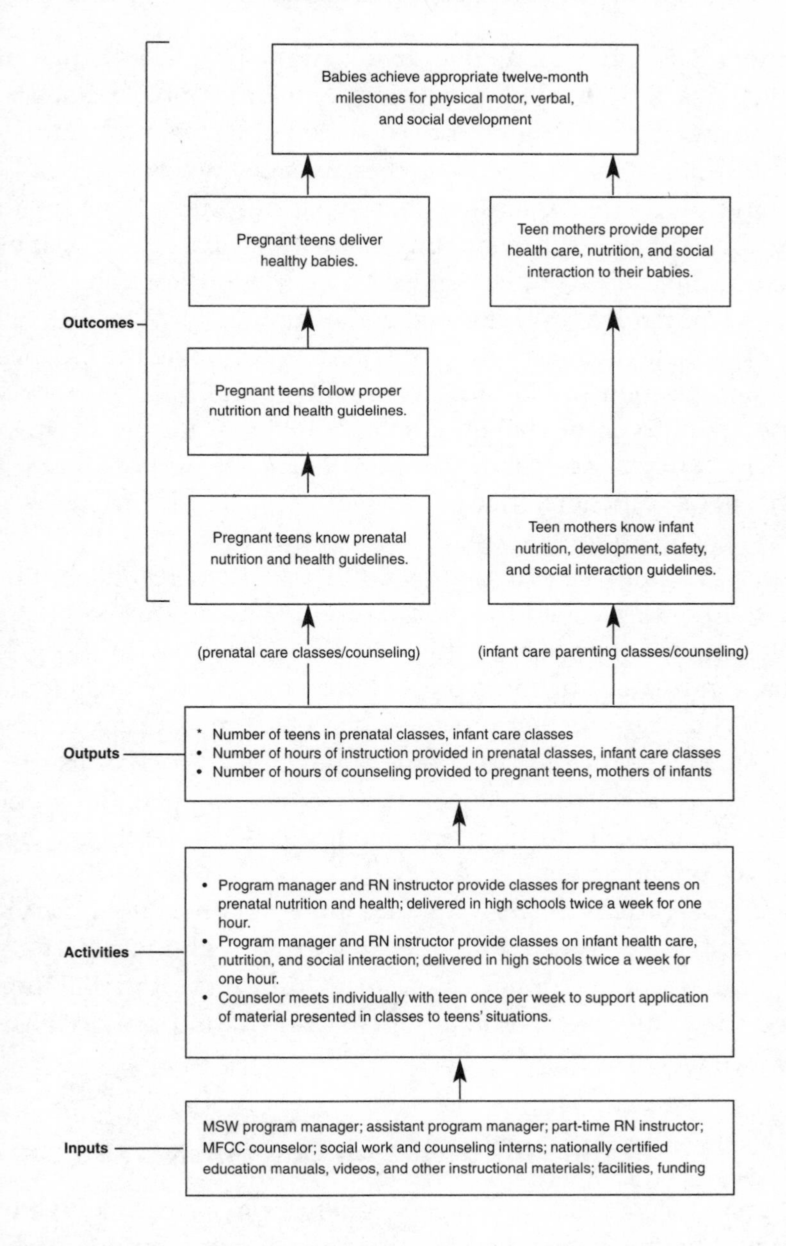

Source: United Way of America, 2002. Us Used by permission.

Minding the Gap

Strategy maps and logic models are useful tools in measuring public outcomes. But they do not necessarily tell the public manager if the time and effort that goes into each step of that model ultimately adds public value. For that, the manager needs a means of weighing outcomes, assuming that some outcomes have greater value than others and evaluating how much it costs to achieve those outcomes. The Public Service Value Model complements the Balanced Scorecard by identifying the high-level outcomes that link to all of the organization's strategies. When using the Balanced Scorecard, harried public managers tend to fall back to tracking outputs. However, in choosing metrics that can inform improvements in performance, managers need to choose outputs that lead directly to an outcome. Many times, in practice this link between outputs and outcomes is lost.

A program may be providing socially beneficial results, but if it appears to have reached the point of diminishing returns—that is, if new money being spent on the program is not producing as great a desired result as it had in the past—then the public manager may want to consider whether greater social value might be reaped by directing program funds to another outcome. To accomplish that task, public managers need a new framework like the Public Service Value Model for thinking about policy trade-offs and how to deliver public outcomes.

From the earliest stages, our intentions for the Public Service Value Model is that it should work in concert with other performance management frameworks, in addition to the Balanced Scorecard, including total quality management and activity-based costing (see Figure 2.5).

Putting the Focus on Outcomes

As we have seen, public managers benefit from a clear view of the outcomes that their organizations need to achieve in order to deliv-

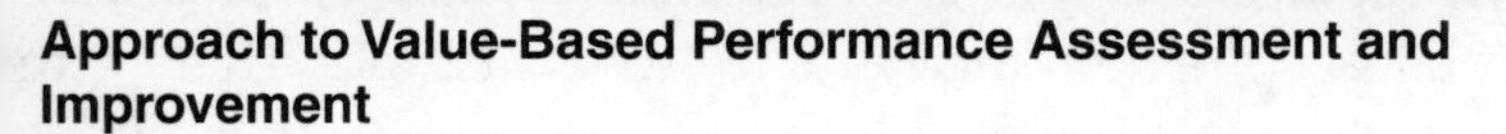

FIGURE 2.5

Approach to Value-Based Performance Assessment and Improvement

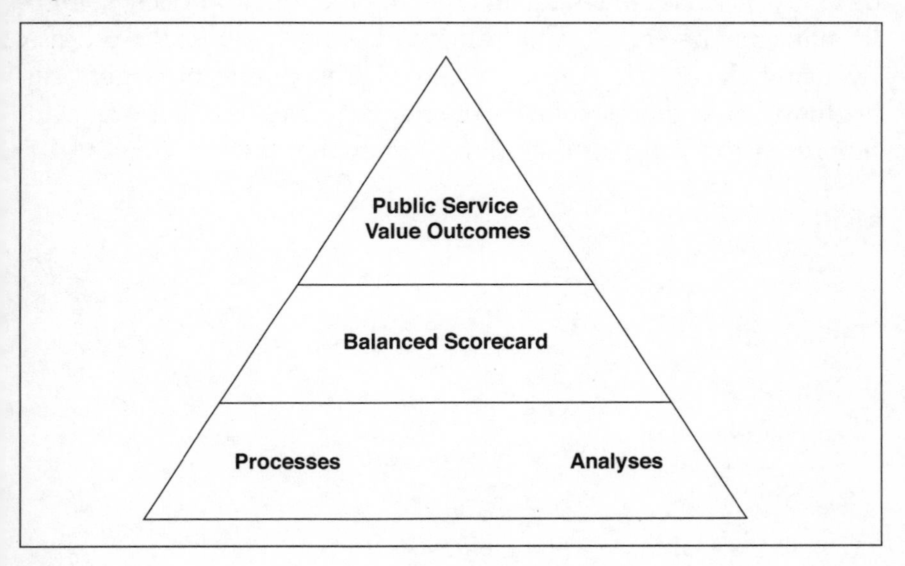

er value to their stakeholders. These outcomes are a combination of the statutory purpose for which the organization exists as well as the expectations of citizen stakeholders. However, outcomes can be slippery. On the one hand, they must be general enough to capture the full scope of an organization's purpose but on the other hand, they must be measurable—at least by proxy—if they are to be of any use in determining whether public value has in fact been created or destroyed. And they have to recogize that different stakeholders—citizens, taxpayers, services users and politicians—can have different perceptions of value at different times.

A key innovation of the Public Service Value Model is to propose some simple and robust techniques for identifying and measuring outcomes. These techniques are discussed in Chapter 4 and described in further detail in the Appendix, but in summary, they are built around an outcomes filter, which helps to identify an organization's key outcomes, and a metrics filter, which ensures that the metrics chosen are both measurable and actionable. There can be many obstacles to taking an outcome-focused approach, so public managers need tools and frameworks to help guide the process. By using the Public Service Value Model, public managers can begin to assess more explicitly the public value that their organizations are producing for the public money that they spend.

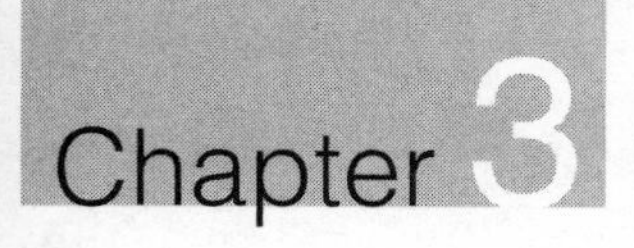

Why Is It So Hard to Measure Public Value?

Attempts to measure public value face formidable obstacles. Measuring outcomes is difficult, and reliable outcome data are sometimes not readily available. In some cases, technology can be a useful tool for public managers to manage data collection. Other complexities in measuring public value include dealing with the unintended consequence of certain metrics, accounting for the results of public-private partnerships and recognizing that outcomes often are shared between multiple organizations. The good news is that the actual process of deciding on what outcomes to measure may contribute to overcoming resistance to using outcomes and lead to healthy discussions.

Even the most effective government agencies may find it difficult to measure their "bottom line" contribution to public value. Spain's social security agency, the Instituto Nacional de la Seguridad Social (INSS), was an early adopter of performance measurement techniques, having developed an outcome tracking model in the 1980s. The agency is widely praised for its level of customer service compared with other national agencies, and among its European peers. Spain's leading political parties pledged in 1995 to support what became known as the Toledo Agreement, promising that they would not tamper with the social security system in order to achieve a short-term political gain. Ten years and three governments later, the agreement is still holding.[1]

Yet the agency realized in mid-2004 that for all its experience with performance measurement and customer focus, it was having trouble measuring just how it was adding public value. The INSS found itself wrestling with how to measure a key outcome in mid-2004: How was the agency getting closer to the citizen? It did not have any consistently reliable information on who was coming into its nearly 300 offices around the country and who was tapping its Internet web site for information.[2] Like many government agencies, the INSS was confident it was adding value, but it lacked the ability to measure the "bottom line" equivalent outcome of the multiple ways in which it was establishing a closer relationship with its citizen stakeholders.

You Get What You Measure

Mark Howard spent a decade beginning in the mid-1980s serving in city management for three different municipalities in the United States—Carrolton, Texas, just outside Dallas; Longmont, Colorado, near Denver; and Baraboo, Wisconsin, north of Madison. Not once, he recalled, did he ever come across anything close to a "bottom line" with which to measure local government value. "There was no simple bottom line for government. You had to pull information from dozens if not hundreds of sources to see if you were adding value or not. Even the question of whether or not you were adding value was often subject to debate; one person's helpful service was another person's waste of tax money. And remember, these were relatively small, more manageable, less politically charged cities," added Howard.

The difficulty in measuring value in public service organizations is not the mere lack of a share price; it is the reason why, in public services, there cannot be a true price at all. Government is not in the business of seeking an economic profit. Rather, it is in the business of delivering various *public goods* whose actual value to stakeholders cannot be easily expressed in monetary terms. How can you calculate the actual "price" of a life saved by preventing a public health outbreak through the administration of existing vaccinations? Or of a neighborhood's increased sense of safety because of municipal street lighting? In a profit-seeking organization, all activity ultimately can be expressed in monetary terms, including the price of individual goods and services. In public services, this translation into purely monetary terms cannot be done in a satisfactory and standard way, either for the individual or for the public as a whole. Hence the need for an alternative way to measure value.

Over the past few decades, common wisdom has championed that easy-to-understand performance measurements and goals drive superior performance. The "bottom line" in business is a clearly understood measure of private sector performance. The search for a similar performance measure for public service organizations and the desire to improve performance in general terms have driven a great deal of public-sector research around the world.

Traditionally, governments have found it easier and more straightforward to measure inputs, processes and outputs when gauging their performance, rather than to focus on outcomes. After all, outcomes may take several years to fully play out, while public managers and policymakers may be more focused on shorter-term election cycles and interim results. In addition, the public service organization trying to achieve an end outcome is most likely not the only entity that can influence it. Police forces can set "reducing crime" as an outcome, yet unemployment rates, household income and educational achievement, not to mention effective locks and burglar alarms, are all factors that may influence crime rates, yet are beyond the managerial control of any police force.

Difficulties Measuring Public Service Value

Why is it so hard to measure value in the public sector? As we have seen, the public sector lacks a single "bottom line," as in private sector profit, which is comparable across different types of public service organizations and different countries around the world. Public sector performance data also usually lack uniform reliability and availability. It is difficult to compare performance across governments or institutions that operate in different socioeconomic environments and contexts. And even within a single government there are typically myriad ways of measuring value.

Even if it is clear what to measure, data collection can be tough in public service organizations. "At the federal agency level there is often a lack of comparable information. They don't do a good job collecting data to measure how they're doing," said Brian Riedl, a budget analyst with the Heritage Foundation. This data collection shortfall was not deliberately designed to thwart progress in performance measurement, Riedl noted. It simply is a reflection of many far-flung bureaucracies that have developed different systems over time without much thought given to coordinated measurements.

Indeed, a 50-state Public Service Value study of U.S. child support agency performance by Accenture found that reliability issues around data provided by certain states to the federal government tended to undermine the value of state-by-state comparisons. "There were too many one-trick ponies, or categories where a single metric within a given state's data was so out of line with other trends that it had an outsized weight on the final results," said George Chaplin one of the principal architects of the study. He added that it "made more sense to look at the nationwide summary data." Summary data across the 50-state agencies in the Public Service Value analysis suggested that child support collections and other outcomes had dramatically increased nationwide following the enactment of enabling legislation in 1996. The study also found a corollary increase in expenditures during the same period, which were necessary to implement the enacted legislative requirements.

Most past efforts to measure public value have been focused internally, on the organization, rather than externally, on citizen stakeholders. "The public sector is struggling to look at an array of measures, financial and nonfinancial, to measure value," noted Gartner Group analyst David McClure. "A problem over the last decade is that value efforts largely have been internally focused on operational efficiencies and ignored citizen or stakeholder benefits," he added. As Harvard University Lecturer in Public Policy, Robert Behn, observed in the September–October 2003 issue of *Public Administration Review*, "All of the reliable and valid data about performance is of little use to public managers if they lack a clear idea about how to use them or if the data are not appropriate for this particular use."[3]

Clearing High-Tech Hurdles

One issue holding back performance measurement over the years has been the difficulty in collecting data from disparate systems and "crunching" it in a timely, cost-effective and useful manner. Recent advances in hardware and software and the plunging price of digital storage capacity, among other factors, has alleviated, or at least lowered, many of these potential hurdles. Henry Fleming, a senior executive with Accenture's Information Management Services unit, works with clients to implement business intelligence software packages that organize and present metrics and enable a user to quickly identify trends and relationships. He noted that "Historically, the downside of many so-called balanced scorecard programs has been a tendency to rationalize the number of metrics and the refresh frequency, resulting in a fractional and infrequent view of business performance. That was the doctrine rolled out about 10 years ago. Since then, intranets have become ubiquitous; commercial software solutions have become plentiful; and storage has become cheap. These factors have *rapidly* enabled comprehensive, virtually real-time intelligence solutions. We will see these solutions become as essential to the CEO as they are for the warehouse manager by 2008." The technology has gotten to the point now where gathering the information is not nearly as painful as it used to be.

Public service organizations around the world have increasingly been using the Internet to post and share performance information. Such information sharing is often helpful and can lead to new insights based on managers in one country or region seeing different approaches being pursued by managers elsewhere. The problem is that in most cases the shared data lack consistency or a common denominator that allows for meaningful comparisons across organizations.

A handful of examples demonstrate the range of performance information that is available online. The New Zealand federal government posts a great deal of performance measurement information online. In the United Kingdom, local metrics are readily available. In the United States, reams of data from all levels of government can be downloaded from federal web sites about the results of the President's Management Agenda, to the "Grade the States" initiative with information on state performance, to New York City's "My

Neighborhoods" program (see Figure 3.1). The My Neighborhoods web site allows the user to designate a street address or intersection, and then view a selection of law enforcement, education, social service and other statistics for the surrounding neighborhood.

Unintended Consequences

Another difficulty with measuring outcomes in the public sector is that sometimes metrics that benefit citizens in one respect may have unintended consequences that can do more harm than good.

FIGURE 3.1

New York City's My Neighborhood Statistics Program

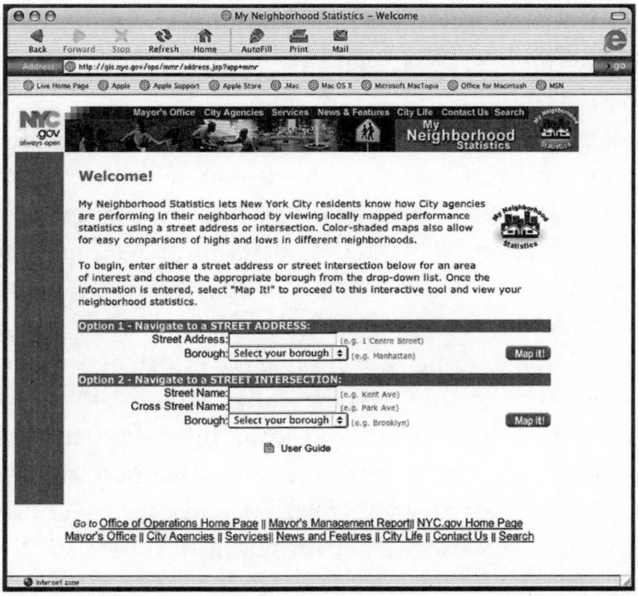

It is critical to investigate what behavior is encouraged by a given metric and to ask whether or not that behavior is in line with the intended outcome.

Call centers often face mismeasurement issues. Metrics created to measure call center efficiency typically give operators targets of 60, 90 or 120 seconds in which to complete a call and be ready to handle another. Although that target is aimed at boosting operator productivity, it might actually encourage operators to transfer "problem" calls to another department or to even hang up on the caller. By focusing measurement on a target time, rather than on satisfactorily dealing with the concerns of the customer on the phone, the measure does not give the operator the incentive to improve the real intended outcome of the call center—satisfied customers. Such metrics may also reflect deeper issues. If the goal is to address citizen problems on the first call to a call center, then there must be sufficient investment and training in the operators so that they have the information and technology available at their fingertips to accomplish that goal.

Public service organizations may also find that emphasizing, or sometimes over-emphasizing, one outcome may have the unintended consequence of under-emphasizing the importance of another outcome.

Revenue agencies may find, for example, that allocating a greater amount of resources to customer service can greatly improve the outcome of minimizing taxpayer burden. Yet if care is not taken, the agency may find that its improved customer satisfaction has come at the expense of another outcome, such as maximizing compliance, if resources are shifted away from audit and related functions to fund the increased effort at improving customer service. The Public Service Value Model provides a framework that executives can use to explicitly weigh up the balance between potentially conflicting outcomes by encouraging them to formulate more creative strategies that will improve multiple outcomes without significantly diminishing others. By targeting audits and thereby minimizing the number of unwarranted audits, for example, the overall burden on compliant taxpayers is reduced.

Measuring Public-Private "Networks"

In many countries, a further challenge for public managers is to find ways to measure, and manage, new public-private "networks," according to Stephen Goldsmith, the former mayor of Indianapolis and current director of the Innovations in American Government Program at Harvard's Kennedy School. In *Governing by Network: The New Shape of the Public Sector* (December 2004), Goldsmith and William Eggers, a senior fellow at the Manhattan Institute for Policy Research, point out that the U.S. federal government currently spends more annually on outside contracts than it does for employee payroll. Among U.S. agencies that are especially geared toward private contracting, "NASA and the Department of Energy both spend more than 80 percent of their respective budgets on contracts," the authors note.[4]

To adequately measure and manage these public-private networks, government managers need to redefine their typical top-down approach to management, the authors say. Managers should focus instead on contract negotiations, contract management and risk analysis, in addition to more traditional planning and budgeting functions. Goldsmith and Eggers note that governments would benefit from viewing such networks as temporary or semi-permanent partnerships.

In public-private ventures, as much as in purely private or purely public service organizations, it is incumbent on executives to justify programs by their added value. The Public Service Value methodology can be useful to executives of public-private networks because it offers a rigorous and structured approach to determine the overall goals and outcomes of the joint enterprise and then to design partnership contracts so that incentives are in place for all parties to achieve those outcomes.

Complexity of Measuring Shared Public Outcomes

Private sector performance measures tend to focus on quarterly and yearly results that, when translated into a net profit or loss statement, provide management with a report card on the company's performance. The corporate sector is often criticized for taking such a relatively short-term view of organizational performance. That said, there is no question that the rigors of private sector financial reporting—though not immune to fraudulent behavior, as recent scandals attest—force myriad corporate activities to be reduced to a single performance measure of value.

The public sector, lacking a bottom line per se, has a much harder time adequately measuring value. The difficultly in measuring value increases dramatically in the case of governments or public sector institutions tackling especially complex social issues. For example, a social program focused on getting unemployed parents back into the workforce may grapple with issues that cross the institutional boundaries of the government and nonprofit agencies that are serving the needs of the previously unemployed. Training and/or education for the job seeker, child care for their children and transportation to and from work are just some of the needs that the network of social services agencies has to meet in order to accomplish the goal of getting the unemployed back to work.

Then there is the issue of cause and effect. To use the above example, it would be extremely difficult to determine whether the efforts of the social services network were the primary reason for getting someone successfully back to work, or whether a booming local economy suddenly provided the right type of job. Most likely, a mix of causes, some driven by public sector programs and training, and some due to jobs being created in the private sector, is responsible for the outcome. Measuring that mix and distinguishing between cause and effect is extremely difficult and usually involves shared outcomes between multiple organizations.

The legitimate emphasis that many politicians give to getting elected or reelected, especially those who face elections every few years, can compress the time frame for adding public value. Many factors contribute to creating value over time, but few long-term gains may be attainable during an average legislative tenure of two, four or even five years. The Public Service Value methodology's approach to framing issues around short- and long-term outcomes gives forward-looking politicians a way of seeking and articulating the big picture to constituents. If politicians can rally constituents behind longer-term outcomes like public health and community safety, they may also be able to convince voters that they are best suited to lead government toward those outcomes over time.

Finally, the time frame under which most public service organizations operate is vastly different than in the private sector, even if public sector funding tends to be tied to annual budgets. Getting the unemployed onto the job rolls, and keeping them there, is a multiyear undertaking, as is providing care for their children. Programs to reduce unemployment could hardly be said to have added value if the participants lost their jobs within a year or two of getting them, or as soon as the economy entered a recession.

Public managers know that multiple organizations in the same or related fields actually share outcomes. In such cases, becoming high-performance organizations requires teamwork to determine which organization pursues which goal in order to avoid or at least limit duplicative behavior. One approach to dealing with shared outcomes is to have each organization distinguish between its short-, mid-, and long-term outcomes. Typically, short- and mid-term outcomes are within the sphere of influence of an organization or an electoral term. Long-term outcomes, however, usually lie outside of any one agency's or government's sphere of influence. Leaders are often reluctant to measure long-term outcomes because of a concern for being held accountable for results that are beyond their immediate control. By focusing on controllable outcomes, it becomes easier to address the issue of shared accountability.

Employment, or reducing unemployment, as we have seen above, is an example of a shared outcome. Reducing the number of unemployed people is the key long-term outcome shared by government labor agencies around the world; however, unemployment levels are driven by multiple factors, such as macroeconomic trade imbalances, education levels and corporate investment, which are beyond the direct reach of labor agencies. Labor agencies instead tend to focus on intermediate-term outcomes, such as matching job seekers with available jobs. Fulfilling this intermediate outcome in turn contributes to meeting the ultimate outcome of reducing unemployment (see Figure 3.2).

Although pubic managers tend to target what is readily measurable (i.e. inputs, processes and outputs), a growing number of governments are focusing their public services organizations on achievement of citizen-oriented outcomes, rather than on simply "meeting their (readily measurable) targets." Making the transition to an outcome-oriented organization is a matter of acknowledging both the shift in what is being measured, as well as the broader questions about what is driving performance.

One example of an agency that has recently begun this transformation into an outcome-oriented organization is the Finnish

FIGURE 3.2

Public Service Value Outcomes: Short-Term, Intermediate-Term and Long-Term

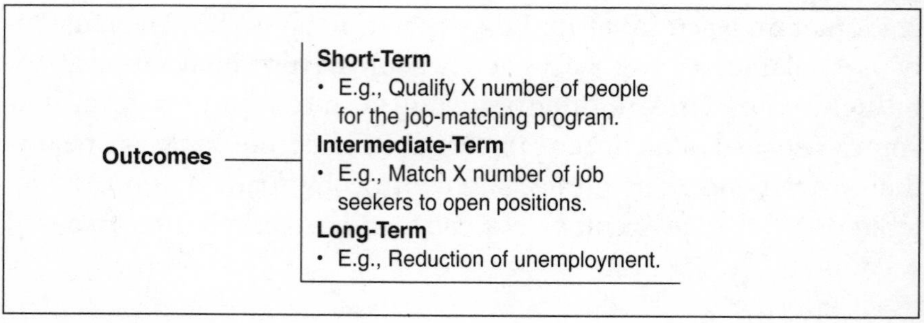

Outcomes

Short-Term
- E.g., Qualify X number of people for the job-matching program.

Intermediate-Term
- E.g., Match X number of job seekers to open positions.

Long-Term
- E.g., Reduction of unemployment.

Directorate of Immigration, which handles one of the most far-reaching cross-boundary processes in the Finnish government. The Directorate, under the Finnish Ministry of Interior, works in close cooperation with many other groups on immigration matters, including the Police, the Frontier Guard, the Ministry for Foreign Affairs, the Ministry of Labour, reception centres for asylum seekers, the Ombudsman for Minorities, the Ministry of Trade and Industry, education authorities, the Centre for International Mobility, the Ministry of Justice and the court system.

When Jorma Vuorio was nominated to be the Director-General of the Directorate in 2004, the challenges of cross-agency cooperation were evident. Customer-facing processes were quite time consuming. For example, residence permits were granted in approximately 3 months, asylum seekers waited around 10 months, and citizenship applicants waited an average 3 years for their cases to be decided. The new Director-General proceeded to implement a transformation program aimed at developing seamless cross-agency processes utilizing a modern case management system. However, he knew that process and systems improvements alone would not solve the cooperation challenge.

At the same time, stakeholder expectations toward immigration outcomes were mounting. The number of foreign born citizens living in the country increased from 20,000 in 1990 to 114,000 in 2005 (about 2% of the population). And the Finnish private sector needed increasing numbers of international talent due to an acute shortage of local skilled labor. The government added pressure by developing a challenging new immigrations policy. As the central operative agency responsible for immigration issues, the Directorate of Immigration bore the heaviest expectations. Yet without any vertical performance management system, the Directorate had little direct influence over its cooperation partners, nor the outcomes it was expected to produce.

As a result, the Directorate's leadership pulled together top executives from the seven government organizations involved in the immigrations process to define a shared understanding of the value delivered by the cross-agency process. The group created a shared outcome model that consists of four outcomes: optimizing fairness and equity, offering international protection, enabling demand-based and smooth transition of foreign workforce into the labor market and ensuring security of immigration. No single ministry or organization is able to deliver any of these outcomes alone, and at the same time, most of the organizations involved bear a shared responsibility for more than one outcome.

It was the process of defining tasks, structures and outputs that helped the participants figure out the concrete value delivery logic of the cross-agency process. And the Public Service Value approach provided a structured framework for fitting the pieces together. While the Directorate's transformation into an outcome-orientated agency is still in its early stages, its efforts—along with the other agencies—to define and measure shared outcomes was a critical first step on the path to improving immigration outcomes.

Improvements in Police Performance

The Greater Manchester Police (GMP) was challenged to improve performance in investigating and detecting crime. The force had been getting unwelcome recognition for its underperformance; for example, its jurisdiction consistently ranked below average in terms of domestic burglary and robbery crimes when compared with similar police forces. GMP already had access to the United Kingdom's Policing Performance Assessment Framework (PPAF), a robust performance measurement and management system, similar to the Public Service Value Model, that focuses on outcomes and efficiency and allows for detailed analysis and comparison of performance. Now it had to develop and implement a framework that would move the force from simply measuring performance to taking actions that would appreciably improve the job it was doing.[5]

GMP led an assessment of its existing organizational and operational capabilities, ranging from its vision and strategy all the way to its training and development programs, that laid the groundwork for prioritizing initiatives, and became the basis for an improvement program along three lines: process, people and data.

The rigor of PPAF paid off. The initiatives GMP put in place have seen lead indicator performance improve across numerous process areas. Indicator data are now used to support operational managers and staff in assessing local performance and, in an important corollary, staff can now be held accountable for good and bad performance against the activities that they directly impact and manage. Overall, GMP's performance in absolute terms, and in relation to its "family" of most similar forces, is improving.

Overcoming Resistance

Even the best-laid plan to focus on citizen-defined outcomes can meet resistance. The resistance may come from within the public service organization itself. Public managers, conscious of the politics that often play a key role in the appropriation or budgeting process, may worry that an outcome focus will have a negative impact on long-established political backing for many well-accepted outputs.

While a switch to outcomes can encounter institutional resistance, it also can, and often does, provide opportunities for strategic discussions that can help overcome institutional logjams. Recently, a new director was named head of a U.S. federal government acquisitions department. The new director viewed the development of public service outcomes and metrics as crucial to building department morale and "buy in" from senior staff. Prior to this exercise, he was challenged to define clearly the department's mission and vision. He had his team of senior staff meet as a group and take ownership of the outcome development process in a workshop setting. He did not state his own preferences until the group had been given an opportunity to debate what they thought were the outcomes they should target to help them become a high-performance organization—a debate that built understanding and commitment.

The process of focusing on outcomes can also enable meaningful deliberation among decision makers on how to improve health system performance. Ontario's Ministry of Health and Long Term Care (MOHLTC) retained Accenture in the spring of 2005 to use the Public Service Value methodology to help with the information management portion of its transformation agenda, which we will discuss in more detail in a later chapter. The process of assigning weightings to proposed Public Service Value outcomes brought together the top leadership at the MOHLTC to focus on possible policy trade-offs in the Ministry's direction as they envisioned the future funding priorities for the health sector.

What the Public Service Value Model Brings to the Table

As we have seen, the problem with measuring value in the public sector is that there is no "bottom line" because there is no common denominator in which both outcomes and costs can be rendered. This makes measuring public value a complex task. If public value concepts are to be useful as management and planning tools, techniques are needed to enable public managers to assess public value in a robust and reliable but not overly complex way. This is an important innovation that the Public Service Value Model provides. The Public Service Value methodology is an approach that public managers can use to measure public value and to identify actionable insights to improve value delivery.

Taking Stock

Let us take a moment to review what we have covered in these first three chapters, and what we will be addressing in the following chapters. In the initial chapters, we focused on the need for public value. We discussed the need for a new approach to public sector performance measurement based on the "value squeeze" confronting public managers worldwide as they are expected continually to do more with less. We then addressed the increasing focus on outcomes in the public sector and how difficult it is to measure outcomes, as compared with the more traditional yardsticks—inputs and outputs.

In the next three chapters, we will shift to a "how-to" focus on implementing the Public Service Value methodology. In Chapters 4 through 6 we address how public managers can apply the Public Service Value Model to public service organizations. We examine in particular the process of defining value and analyzing and measuring results, walking through the steps involved in performing a Public Service Value analysis. The final chapter focuses on innovation and how it can be used to unlock public value.

Chapter 4

Defining Value

Determining what to measure in order to gauge whether an organization is adding value is central to the Public Service Value methodology. We introduce our definition of public value and present a practical methodology for defining outcomes and selecting outcome-oriented metrics. We will also see that organizations do not need to start from scratch, but can take a first step by filtering the metrics that they already collect to identify the ones that tie directly or indirectly to outcomes. The selection process includes filtering the outcomes and metrics and assigning weights to each.

The U.K. government under Prime Minister Tony Blair is in the midst of a multiyear effort to "drive up the value of services and policies to citizens and drive down the costs," said Ian Watmore, head of the Prime Minister's Delivery Unit. In order to do this, Blair's government cut tens of thousands of administrative support and related jobs and will relocate more than 20,000 additional public sector employees out of London and the southeast of England to less expensive locations by 2010. At the same time, the government has been focusing much more intently on outcomes such as better access to health care, higher educational attainment for broader portions of society and higher throughput of the traffic network, rather than looking at traditional measures of inputs and outputs.[1]

What the U.K. government is still trying to figure out is how to measure the extent to which it is adding public value every day. "We don't have a way of measuring the value improvement," said Watmore. "We are looking at it. We don't have the answers yet. This government is focusing on how to get the value felt by ordinary people," he added. Because the Public Service Value approach looks at public outcomes from the perspective of stakeholders, like "ordinary people," using this methodology helps give governments a way to make value come alive for constituents.

What to Measure

Deciding what to measure to determine whether an organization is creating value is an essential component of the Public Service Value methodology. And often the decision is less than clear-cut. The results of performance measurement exercises are colored by what is measured. By the same logic, if we go to the trouble of measuring outcomes, we are much more likely to achieve them.

Restructuring government services is often more straightforward than determining whether and how the restructured service may be adding value. While going through an extensive reorganization of state health and human service agencies and functions, the State of Texas was federally required to release a request for proposal for Texas's Medicaid claims and primary care case management services. A team led by ACS and supported by Accenture won the bidding for that multiyear contract in 2003, and took over claims processing in January 2004 under the name of the Texas Medicaid and Healthcare Partnership (TMHP). By the end of 2004, TMHP leadership was ready to review TMHP's progress and talk about long-term strategic planning.

A small team working at TMHP looked to the Public Service Value Model for guidance in assessing the performance of the program and charting a path forward. The basis for their evaluation was a 50-state study of U.S. Medicaid agencies that used the Public Service Value methodology. The nationwide Public Service Value study measured state Medicaid agencies' success in achieving three broad outcomes: (1) maximize utilization of preventive services; (2) maximize access; and (3) optimize revenue and medical costs. The team at TMHP agreed that these outcomes dovetailed with the Texas Health and Human Services Commission's mission for the Medicaid Program. But the three outcomes were not sufficient. In order to address another important aspect of the Texas Medicaid Program's mission, the team wanted to include an additional outcome to measure progress toward achieving the goal of providing improved service to providers in order to retain them in the Medicaid system. So they added a fourth outcome: minimize administrative burden.

Based on these four outcomes, a Public Service Value analysis was conducted that revealed that from fiscal years 2001 to 2004 the Texas Medicaid Program had experienced steady and consistent progress each year. The gains for fiscal 2004 were particularly striking in the minimize administrative burden area. The gains were due in part to innovations TMHP put in place, including new call center technology, improved claims adjudication processes and a new web portal for health care providers. The Public Service Value analysis showed that the agency was able to add value by meeting the health needs of citizens as well as reducing the time and effort providers had to devote to administrative issues.

Defining Public Service Value

What do we mean by the term *public service value*? By our definition, public service value is about more than simply attaining outcomes, and it is about more than just reducing cost; it is about doing both in a balanced fashion and understanding the strategic trade-offs available along the way. In the next chapter, we will examine in detail how to use the Public Service Value Model to evaluate performance. But first let us understand what the Public Service Value Model measures.

The Public Service Value methodology measures how well an organization, or series of organizations, achieves outcomes and cost-effectiveness year after year (see Figure 4.1). The methodology gives public managers a way to evaluate an organization's performance in relationship to the organization's average performance over a series of years. (The methodology uses the concept of an "average year" so that an organization can make different base units comparable. We go into this topic in detail in Chapter 5 when we discuss normalization.)

Public managers need to consider their relative performance in

FIGURE 4.1

Public Service Value Model

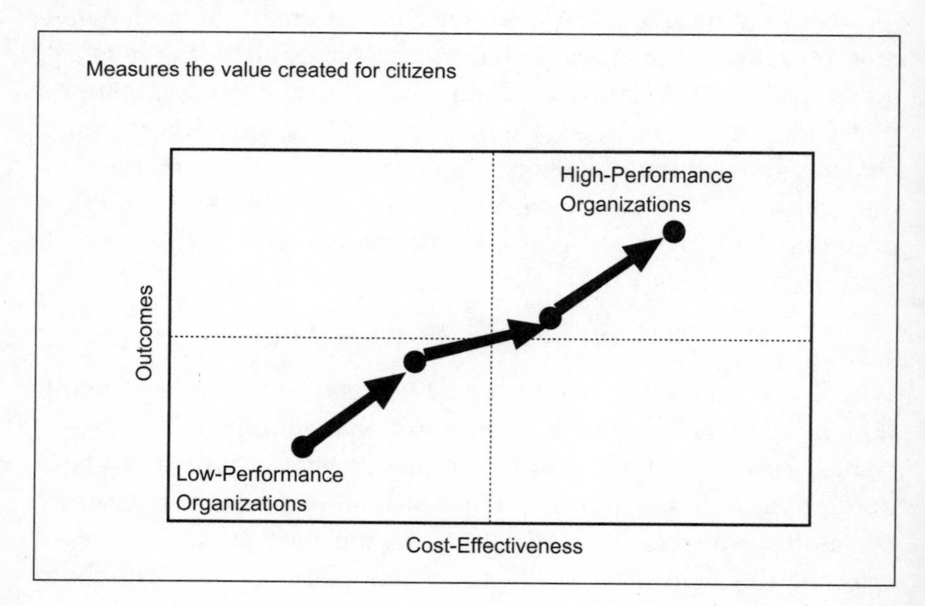

the context of a larger group of similar organizations. For instance, if a hypothetical city decreased its annual traffic fatality rate from 90 to 80 people per year, that would appear to represent significant value added in terms of outcomes. But if the national average for city-wide traffic fatalities was only 10 per year, that would cast the "progress" of that particular city in a different light, which managers would need to consider. Either contributing conditions in that particular city were dramatically unusual and need addressing or performance was not as good as it could have been. As more data from the use of Public Service Value methodology becomes available and more widespread across the public sphere, we expect to develop greater ability to promote these comparative assessments in future.

Outcomes: Public Service Value's North Star

Choosing the right set of outcomes is crucial to the success of using the Public Service Value methodology. The outcome model is a public service organization's North Star. It is the organization's ultimate goal, and even though an organization may tack back and forth during any particular year, the outcomes are still there for it to use as a guide at all times.

Private sector organizations tend to focus on measuring activities or processes that result in increased profits and increased shareholder value. With the Public Service Value Model, value is defined as producing a basket of outcomes desirable to stakeholders and doing so cost-effectively. For example, police departments might aim to achieve outcomes such as reducing crime and increasing the perception of public safety. Likewise, desirable outcomes for a health care organization include improving the health of a population based on a range of yardsticks such as infant mortality rates, incidence of obesity, diabetes, heart disease and so forth. Measuring outcomes that meet citizen expectations is an integral part of the Public Service Value methodology.

Are We There Yet?

Traditional performance measures are analogous to monitoring a car driving down a highway to determine how the car is running. To measure inputs, or the resources used to deliver products or services, we might measure the gallons of gasoline consumed by the car. To measure processes or activities, we might record the miles traveled. And to measure outputs, or the final products, goods, or services produced, we might calculate fuel efficiency in terms of miles traveled per gallon of gasoline consumed. These measurements would all be accurate and provide a good view of the car's performance, but they would not tell much about the journey as a whole. For instance, the car may be performing flawlessly, but if it is on the wrong freeway headed in the wrong direction, the best-performing car in the world will not arrive at the desired destination. Plus, whatever the fuel-efficiency is, the driver will have needlessly spent money on gasoline getting to a destination he was not trying to reach.

The Public Service Value methodology measures short-term, intermediate-term and long-term outcomes. Using the Public Service Value Model to analyze the same car's trajectory, we would measure whether the outcome is achieved—in this example, did the car reach its intended destination in a safe and cost-effective way? Having the most fuel-efficient car in the world, a goal of traditional measurement approaches does not do much good if the car does not get where it needs to go. Similarly, if an organization falls short of achieving an outcome, the Public Service Value analysis provides an assessment of the gap between the goal and reality. Focusing on the reason we got in the car in the first place—to reach our destination—underscores the importance of the Public Service Value Model's focus on outcomes.

Building a Public Service Value Outcome Model

Developing a Public Service Value outcome model for a public service organization is a multistep process that starts with defining the building blocks, moves to identifying, filtering and weighting outcomes, and then to identifying, filtering and weighting metrics. We have found that what is crucially important in each of the steps is the thinking and deliberation that application of the model provokes—in most cases, as important as the precise measures it produces.

The first step in developing a Public Service Value outcome model for a public service organization is to define in detail four building blocks (see Figure 4.2):

1. Mission
2. Core functions or capabilities
3. Stakeholders
4. Stakeholders' expectations

FIGURE 4.2

Public Service Value Building Blocks

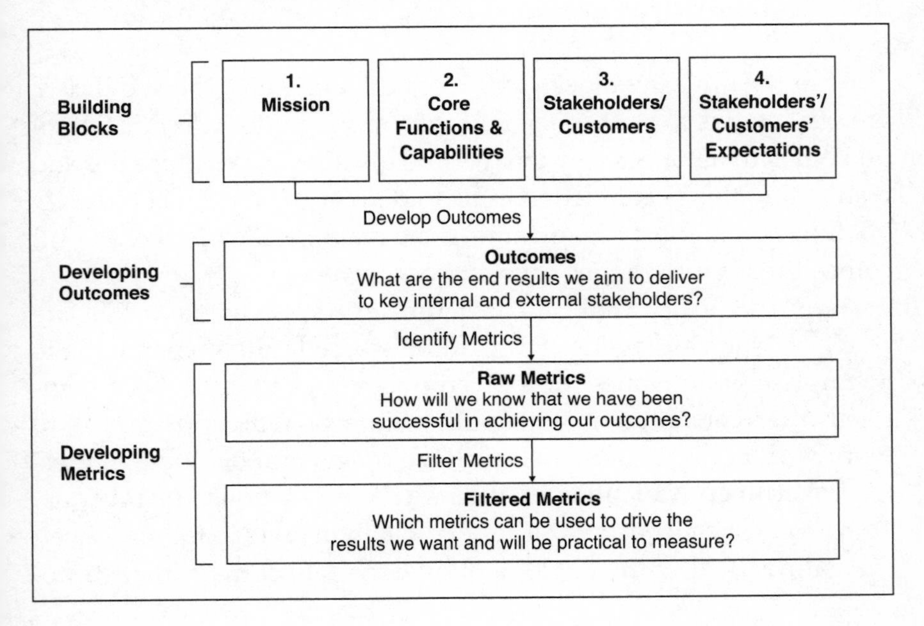

Most public service organizations have a clearly defined mission statement. The mission explains why the organization exists and what would be lost to society if the organization suddenly disappeared. The core functions of an organization are found either in the statutory purpose of a government agency or the bylines of a nonprofit organization. Although there are a range of stakeholders for public service organizations, primacy is given to the taxpayers and beneficiaries of public services. That said, we acknowledge there is no typical taxpayer who represents all public beneficiaries of services. Rather, citizens have diverse views and needs based on their socio-economic background and other factors. The Public Service Value methodology assumes the aggregate view of the citizen but recognizes there is no one archetypical citizen. Stakeholder expectations for different segments can be researched through interviews with public managers as well as more directly through polls, focus groups or other methods of sounding out citizens that are directly and indirectly served by an organization. Ideally, public managers would engage their stakeholders to identify what they want from the organization. In reality, though, this is not often done and surrogate measures of stakeholder demand are used instead.

After the building blocks for an organization have been defined, the next step is to synthesize that information into a description of outcomes that collectively answer the question, "What are the end results that this organization aims to deliver to key stakeholders?" We find that in most organizations, the manageable number of outcomes to measure ranges from three to seven.

As in the Texas Medicaid Program example, where a 50-state study of Medicaid agencies was initially used, often we may have a template of outcomes for a given policy area that has been compiled after consultation with policy experts. Our approach is to work with policy experts to help develop general outcome models for government functions such as Medicaid or police or revenue. Then, for a specific organization, we ask managers to tailor or even substantively alter the outcome models to reflect their own strategic priorities. As noted earlier, when the TMHP team reviewed the Medicaid outcome template, they realized that they needed to add a fourth outcome to measure their ability to achieve the goal of lessening the administrative burden on health care providers.

The 13 areas for which we currently have developed templates of outcome models are listed in Figure 4.3.

As a final check to verify that the outcome development process has succeeded in identifying outcomes that actually reflect the organization's purpose, we use the four-part Public Service Value outcome filter:

1. *Mission Focused*—Is the outcome aligned with the organization's mission and vision?
2. *Action Oriented*—Do the outcomes drive quantifiable improvements? Are employees held accountable for improving outcomes? Do employees understand how their actions affect outcomes?
3. *Comprehensive*—Do the outcomes, taken as a whole, reflect all of the organization's core capabilities, functions and strategies?
4. *Creates Values for Stakeholders*—Is the outcome something that the organization's stakeholders value?

FIGURE 4.3

Public Service Value Outcome Models

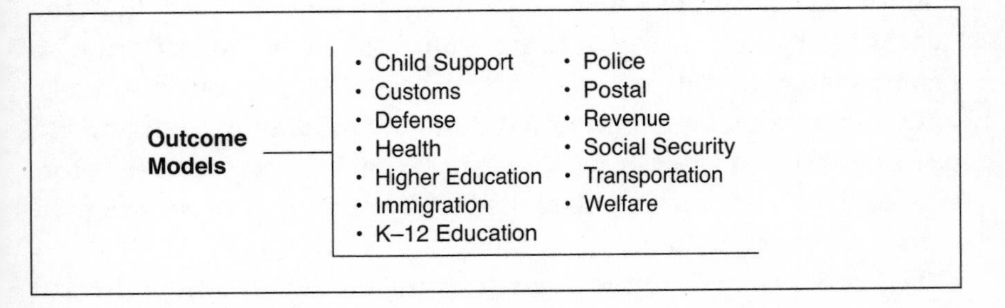

Public service organizations around the world have used this process of developing outcome models to improve performance. For example, when we worked with a cultural institution in Japan, the outcome development methodology helped executives give a renewed focus to the organization's mission, purpose and stakeholders. In San Francisco, we applied the outcome development methodology to The Breakthrough Collaborative, a national nonprofit organization running summer and after-school enrichment programs for underprivileged middle school students. Laura Pochop, Executive Director, said that the Public Service Value methodology "helped focus our work by delineating three groups of stakeholders—our students, teachers and school administrators—and determining the desired outcomes for each group." Additionally, it enabled them to reinforce and enhance their existing performance management efforts. Pochop noted that the nonprofit organization used the Public Service Value Model in concert with a "Balanced Scorecard type report that helps us compare relative performance across the organization and identify best practices at local sites."

At the state and local level, the Public Service Value Model helps an organization keep its focus on key outcomes. John Eckart assumed his position as Commissioner of the Indiana Department of Revenue in February 2005, having previously been President of the Indiana subsidiary of American Water. Eckart, after 30 years in the private sector, saw plenty of similarities in measuring value in both the public and private spheres. And, in fact, Indiana's Department of Revenue undertook a Public Service Value evaluation of its performance in 2003 which demonstrated that the department was clearly adding value in many areas prior to Eckart's arrival. Yet even in such a relatively high-performance government agency, Eckart noted that a lot more work remained to be done: "The concept of viewing the taxpayer as a customer is foreign to the Department. The focus had been more process-oriented than meeting customers' needs."

Figure 4.4 is an example of an outcome model for a hypothetical policing agency.

FIGURE 4.4

Policing Agency Outcome Model and Rationale

Policing Agency

Outcome: Reducing Crime
- **Rationale:** A critical function for police forces is to reduce levels of crime within their area of responsibility. This outcome comprises metrics relating to several different crime types to give a general representation of crime rates.

Outcome: Investigating Crime
- **Rationale:** The police force is responsible for bringing offenders to account for their actions. This outcome measures how successful police forces are in their detection of "victim" crimes, e.g., burglary and robbery.

Outcome: Citizen Focus
- **Rationale:** Citizen focus measures the quality of service provided by police forces. Metrics used are satisfaction ratings of police response when a citizen has been a victim of crime as well as more general public attitudes of the service provided by the police.

Outcome: Promoting Public Safety
- **Rationale:** A key role of the police force is to maintain and promote public safety. This outcome measures the public perception of the level of order/disorder in their community as well as their sense of security.

Identifying Citizen Priorities

Coral Springs, Florida, is a city of roughly 130,000 that is considered one of the most advanced municipalities in the United States in terms of asking citizens directly for their priorities when setting performance goals.[2]

Coral Springs conducts an Annual Citizen Survey to take the population's pulse on a variety of key municipal indicators. The results of the survey play a major role in determining the city's performance goals, or what it calls key intended outcomes. These outcomes and their corresponding metrics are prioritized and are tied to the citizen survey that the city tracks to determine if it is meeting its goals. The city's key intended outcomes, in order of priority, are to maximize:

1. Customer-involved government
2. Neighborhood and environmental vitality
3. Excellence in education
4. Family, youth and community values
5. Financial health and economic development
6. Respect for ethnic and religious diversity

The extent to which each of these intended outcomes is achieved is determined by tracking three to six metrics for each of the intended outcomes (totaling 29 metrics in all). Two-year goals are set for each metric and tracked annually. To take just one example, the six metrics used to track the intended outcome of Customer-involved Government are:

1. Overall quality rating for city services and programs
2. Overall satisfaction rating of city employees
3. Percent of plan reviews completed within 15 days
4. City crime rate (crimes/100,000 residents)—calendar year
5. Quality rating for city employees customer service
6. Percent of voter turnout

Looking at the two-year results for 2003–2004, Coral Springs met or exceeded its goal on 25, or 86 percent, of its metrics. It failed to meet its goals on just three metrics.

Coral Springs has consciously and deliberately put citizen priorities at the center of its planning and budgeting process. Most public sector entities assume that the population they serve is at the center of all their decision-making processes. But this instance illustrates how dramatically a citizen-centric approach to public sector management can reshape government priorities.

Weighting Outcomes

All outcomes may be created equal, but in practice we ask public managers to assign weights on a scale of 100 percent to each of the Public Service Value outcomes to reflect their current strategic priorities. These priorities, in turn, are fundamentally driven by taxpayers' views and politics, and they will vary over time according to changing legislative priorities. One of the benefits of this weighting technique is that it is flexible enough to change with the times. If a new administration comes in with a new direction, the weightings can be reassigned to reflect their priorities. As a result, the value calculations change and the emphasis is placed on differently weighted outcomes. It is not necessary to wait for a change in leadership to reconsider the outcome weightings, however. Rather, it can be done annually as part of a budget process, or when the organization's strategic plan is being updated. It can also be used prospectively to consider what would happen if political priorities or social and economic circumstances change.

For example, at the Arizona Department of Revenue, Director Hibbs' strategy was to focus more on an appropriate balance between tax compliance and customer service, since compliance had not been adequately emphasized in recent years by the department. Director Hibbs tailored the department's outcome model to reflect his desire to create the right balance by weighting the maximize tax revenue and maximize compliance rates highest as seen below.

Arizona Department of Revenue Outcome Model Weights and Rationale in 2003

- *Maximize Tax Revenue (30%).* The most fundamental function of a revenue agency is to administer tax laws fairly and efficiently by collecting appropriate taxes from citizens and businesses.

- *Maximize Compliance Rates (30%).* An increase in the number of taxpayers filing voluntarily and correctly indicates that the revenue agency is being effective with its public outreach, education, customer service and compliance programs.
- *Minimize Taxpayer Burden (20%).* Taxpayers value minimizing the costs of direct and indirect compliance, including the costs associated with filing tax returns (information gathering and submission) and responding to an audit.
- *Maximize Responsiveness to Taxpayers (20%).* Taxpayer responsiveness reflects both the quality of assistance provided by the revenue administration in enabling taxpayers to comply with their legal obligations and the effectiveness of the revenue administration in resolving taxpayer problems.

Not all outcomes that add value might appear at first blush to have a direct link to citizen expectations. Some outcomes are shorter term and closely related to outputs; others are longer term and more closely approximate overall social good. In the case of the Texas Medicaid Program review, the outcomes or goals for which the agency posted the largest percentage increases in value from 2001 to 2004 were (1) minimize administrative burden and (2) optimize revenue and medical costs. These two shorter-term outcomes involve claims processing, recovering funds from third-party insurers and reducing fraud, among other steps. The typical Medicaid client may very well not have been aware of any of these activities.

In addition to defining what constituted outcomes for the Texas

Medicaid Program, the team assigned weights to the four outcomes to express the level of priority. The two outcomes that accounted for 65 percent of the weighting in the model were (1) maximize access (30%) and (2) maximize utilization of preventive services (35%). Indeed, while TMHP and the state plan further enhancements that will make it even easier and faster for providers to work with Medicaid, the long-term focus of the program is to improve health care value by changing the behavior of Medicaid providers and clients.

Texas Medicaid Program Outcome Model Weights and Rationale in 2004

- *Maximize Utilization of Preventive Services (35%).* Use of regular, preventive services reduces the need for interventional high-cost procedures and services, improves the health status of the enrollees and contributes to lower costs in the long run. Lower utilization of high-cost services (e.g. inpatient hospital services) has a similar effect.
- *Maximize Access (30%).* Ensuring that the target population (particularly high-risk groups) is enrolled in Medicaid and has access to necessary services improves health status and reduces cost over time.
- *Optimize Revenue and Medical Costs (20%).* Ensuring all sources of revenue are optimized, including third-party liability and recovery, and tackling fraud, waste and abuse maximizes money available to the program to spend on its core mission of health service delivery.
- *Minimize Administrative Burden (15%).* Streamlining administrative processes improves customer satisfac-

tion and allows providers and the program to focus on health service delivery and on critical initiatives contributing to improved health outcomes over time.

Filtering Metrics

After agreeing to a set of outcomes, the next step to complete an outcome model is to identify, filter and weight metrics that will measure whether or not an outcome is met. One source for identifying metrics is the list of traditional performance metrics and key performance indicators that an organization is already using to track performance. The difference with the Public Service Value methodology is that it does not stop there. Rather, metrics must pass the metrics filter below and answer the question, "Are we achieving our intended outcome?" The metrics filter is useful to identify metrics that can be used to drive desired outcomes and to determine which metrics are also practical to measure. Metrics go through two sets of filters, an intentions filter and a feasibility filter.

1. Intentions filter
    - *Outcome Focused*—Are the metrics measuring the "end goal" of the program or organization and not simply the inputs or outputs used to achieve it?
    - *Customer Focused*—Do the metrics track and measure what customers and other stakeholders' value?
    - *Drives Intended Behavior*—Do the metrics drive the intended behavior?
    - *Actionable*—Does the metric give executives meaningful information to use to make decisions to improve outcomes?
2. Feasibility filter
    - *Measurable*—Are the metrics quantifiable, reliable and well defined?

- *Practical/Affordable*—Do the data currently exist? Is the cost of measurement (time and expenses) justified by the benefit of the measurement?

If metrics that meet the intentions criteria are not readily available or affordable, then organizations often will want to develop proxy metrics. Proxy metrics are available data, or perhaps ratios of existing data, that would measure roughly the same processes as those tracked by the initial metrics. Inverse ratios may also serve as effective proxies for hard-to-attain metrics. A decline in the number of complaints, for example, may serve as a proxy for an increase in customer satisfaction.

Just as we ask public managers to assign weights to the outcomes to make their strategic priorities explicit, we also ask them to assign weights to the metrics for the same purpose. The metric weights can also change over time to reflect changing priorities. Having the discipline to assign weights to each metric and each outcome benefits the organizations in two ways. First, it makes the organization's priorities transparent to stakeholders and managers alike. Secondly, by weighting everything in the outcome model it is possible, as we will see later, to aggregate the metrics data into a type of "total outcome score." But again, more important is the thinking and deliberation that the weighting process provokes.

An example of filtered and weighted metrics used in an outcome model we have already seen is given in Figure 4.5 for the Arizona Department of Revenue.

Cadillac Outcomes, Chevy Budget

Safe Space, a New York nonprofit organization that provides child welfare and foster care services, wanted to get a better sense of how effectively it was meeting its goals. Safe Space administrators contacted Dennis Smith, associate professor of

Figure 4.5

Arizona Department of Revenue Public Service Value Outcome Model

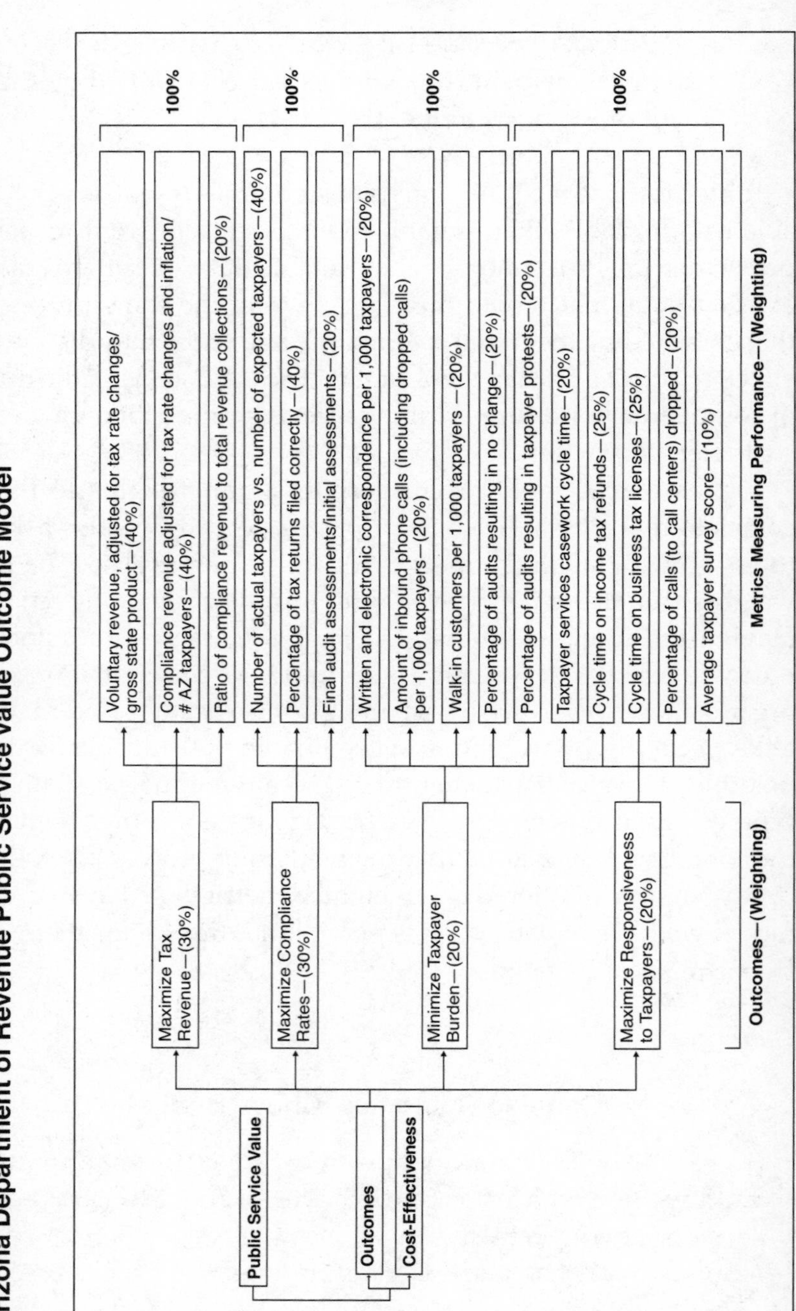

public administration at New York University's Robert F. Wagner Graduate School of Public Service, for help. In 2002, Smith worked with Safe Space to produce a sophisticated performance management methodology, culminating in a logic model, or strategy map, that would help them track their internal performance and focus on achieving program goals or outcomes.

Recently, Safe Space, under new management, contacted Smith again. This time, the nonprofit organization was suffering from too much of a good thing. The logic model had been so useful in tracking their performance and in meeting outcomes that they kept looking for new outcomes to tackle. Each successful program goal, however, while an impressive achievement, was not adequately being tied back into the nonprofit's budget process. They were facing potentially serious budget shortfalls as a result. As Smith recounted, "They were producing Cadillac outcomes with a Chevrolet budget."

He said he especially appreciated the manner in which the Public Service Value Model prompted government or nonprofit administrators to weigh trade-offs between outcomes and cost-effectiveness. "Public Service Value was ahead of us in being able to build in achieving outcomes as cost-effectively as possible," said Smith, noting that he had agreed to go back and help Safe Space make their performance management system more sensitive to cost-effectiveness. When it comes to public sector performance management, added Smith, "Public Service Value is the next step."

Using the Metrics Filter to Decide What to Measure

Using the Public Service Value metrics filter provides a way to check and evaluate whether or not the metrics can give the organization a balanced and holistic assessment of whether or not it is achieving its desired outcomes. The metrics filter also helps cut through the mass of data an organization may collect to identify the few metrics that are needed to tell an organization's performance story.

In most of the Public Service Value analyses that we have conducted, one of the insights that invariably emerges is a list of metrics to be discarded and some new metrics identified that can help the organization focus on its outcomes—on what really matters to the public. Following are a few examples of new outcome-focused metrics that were identified as a result of Public Service Value analyses.

Do Not Forget Service Levels

Spain's social security agency, the Instituto Nacional de la Seguridad Social, developed an outcome tracking model in the 1980s. The benefits agency, which has won several European and national awards for public sector customer service quality, has, apart from multiple other performance measurements, several consolidated systems to analyze and validate the service it provides. This includes citizen satisfaction surveys, which the agency began using in the early 1990s. The citizen-based approach has been a core principle of the agency and has resulted in an increase of the utilization of the agency's citizen centers, as well as improvements in other areas.

However, the agency found itself wrestling with how to measure a key outcome in mid-2004: Was the agency getting closer to the citizen? To answer this question, the agency turned to the Public Service Value methodology. The agency decided to focus on two key outcomes: maximize accessibility and maximize responsiveness. By measuring these two outcomes, the agency would be able to better measure its progress in customer service. In addition, the agency decided to focus on its interactions with citizens over the phone and in its offices in particular since these are the primary vehicles citizens use to interact with the agency.

More Than Just Test Results

In the United Kingdom, the Prime Minister and Department for Education and Skills launched The London Challenge strategy, "Transforming London Secondary Schools" in May 2003. The strategy has three crucial components:

1. Transforming schools in five key London boroughs with particularly low attainment histories
2. Providing support for schools trying to break the link between disadvantage and low attainment
3. Providing a better deal for London students, teachers, leaders and schools

Like many large cities, London has struggled in recent decades to improve conditions in its inner-city schools, many of which have declined in terms of physical condition, student safety and student performance, as income levels in inner city neighborhoods have declined. We conducted a study during the summer of 2005 to determine whether it was possible to "transfer" some of the characteristics of high-performance state-run secondary schools to low-performance schools. Initially based on the five London boroughs identified by the London Challenge initiative, the 25 schools included in the Public Service Value study share similar socio-economic demographic characteristics and were judged to be high performers. This was based on an assessment of teaching methods, governance, the ethos of the school and test results. The schools have a high proportion of students receiving free school meals, with English as an additional language and with poor performance at entry to secondary school.

One of the biggest challenges in the initial phases of the study was to "identify the ideal rather than the traditional outcomes of secondary education," said Jessica Wilson, an Accenture consultant who played a leading role in the project. Higher test scores tended to be the default educational outcome assumed by many education stakeholders. Yet focused discussions with local educational experts and select interviews with teachers, parents and high school students in London led to a significantly different "outcome." Wilson noted that "there was a general consensus that the eventual employability of students is the ultimate outcome, not just test results." To this end, the analysis tracks "soft" metrics such as teamwork, personal responsibility, aspirations, work experience through partnership with local businesses and/or vocational training. The other two key preliminary outcomes identified in the study were to improve the academic experience and the environment of the school and to improve the impact of secondary schools on the broader community.

The key difference between a Public Service Value analysis and the many other studies of value-add in the education sector is the relationship that the Public Service Value methodology draws between outcome performance and cost-effectiveness or "value for money." The high-level value drivers identified by our study included financially literate head teachers and boards who were able to explicitly break the link between the size of a budget allocation and the perceived value that could be generated: vocational qualifications that are aligned to the needs of employers, student security and improved parent trust in the school.

The Public Service Value methodology offers a structured way to define value through outcomes and metrics, which can help public managers focus on an organization's North Star as conditions change and policies shift over time. The process of defining, filtering and assigning weights to outcomes and metrics can be used to bring diverse stakeholders together over what success looks like for a given organization. That in itself can only help improve organizational performance.

Measuring and Analyzing Public Service Value

We start with examining how to get access to the data needed to conduct a Public Service Value analysis and then turn to an in-depth look at how to calculate a Public Service Value score and report the results of an analysis. We will see that the steps to conduct a Public Service Value analysis include calculating outcome and cost-effectiveness scores and then bringing together all the performance data into a Public Service Value matrix. The Public Service Value analysis provides a baseline for evaluating performance by graphically depicting changes in performance.

Equitable access to health care ranks at or near the top of the list of attributes that most Canadians identify as key to their national identity, according to Adalsteinn Brown. His job is to help ensure that the health care system of Ontario, Canada's most populous province, is adding value to make the system not only as equitable as possible, but sustainable as well. In an era of rapidly rising costs and patient expectations, that is a tall order.

Since 2003, Brown has been the Information Management Lead for the Health Results Team—a team made up of executives, academic experts and leaders in the Canadian health care industry appointed by the Ontario Ministry of Health and Long Term Care (MOHLTC) to radically transform the province's health care system.[1] Brown, a 35-year-old native of Ontario with degrees from Harvard and Oxford Universities, was an obvious choice for the job. For the previous five years he had been working with the Ministry and hospitals across the Province to capture health care performance data as the Lead Investigator for the Ontario Hospital Reports Project and was considered a global expert in the field.

Brown had collected copious amounts of performance data, but most of it was in the form of inputs and outputs, and not related to outcomes that reflected health care goals. To capture outcomes, beginning in 2004 Brown and his team began sifting through stacks of planning documents to uncover "revealed strategy" goals, or outcomes, which had not been articulated as such. They also met with systems administrators and interviewed physicians, nurses and other clinicians. Within the first year they identified more than 2,000 metrics that were being collected in the system. That figure was scoped down to 154 through a series of small group meetings, then finally in early 2005 reduced to 27 metrics. There was just one problem, said Brown. "We could not answer whether we were headed in the right direction, whether we were creating a sustainable system." That is where the Public Service Value methodology came in.

Once you know what you want to measure to determine outcomes, finding the information, and employing the Public Service Value Model to determine if the organization is adding value, is the next step. As Brown and his team discovered, it often is not as easy as it sounds. The availability of information, or even the extent to which it has been collected, varies widely among public service entities. Some organizations, with sophisticated information systems and a willingness to collect outcome data, will have most of the information available. Others may require manual data collection. Ultimately, Brown's experience illustrates how the Public Service Value methodology can be used to first sift through reams of metrics, select a useful outcome-oriented data set, collect the necessary data and then conduct an analysis that can tell an organization's "performance story." By focusing on outcomes and not getting lost in the thousands of available metrics, a Public Service Value analysis helps public managers see the big picture.

Data Collection: Metrics Mania

Before diving into how to calculate a Public Service Value score, we will first address the universal issues of how to gather and get access to the data needed to conduct an analysis. The situation Brown and his team encountered at the Ontario MOHLTC is far from an anomaly. Public service organizations regularly track hundreds of metrics, if not more, although few are directly related to outcomes. To an extent, the large number of metrics reflects the size and complexity of the organization being measured (see Figure 5.1), as well as a response to prevailing political demands.

That said, even organizations with a more narrow scope, such as Arizona's Department of Revenue, have suffered from what might be described as metrics overload. For some time, Arizona's Department of Revenue tracked more than 600 performance metrics that covered all of the department's functions and activities. Director Hibbs narrowed the number tracked by his office to a manageable 40 or so, but was still dissatisfied that those measures were persuasive in demonstrating the value provided by the department. Nor did he think the measures would persuade decision makers that investing further in revenue would increase the performance and value of the agency to taxpayers. Undertaking the Public Service Value study in 2003 provided a good approach to not only narrowing the number of critical measures to track, but also to presenting the information in a better way in order to help

Figure 5.1

Size and Complexity of the Ontario Health Care System

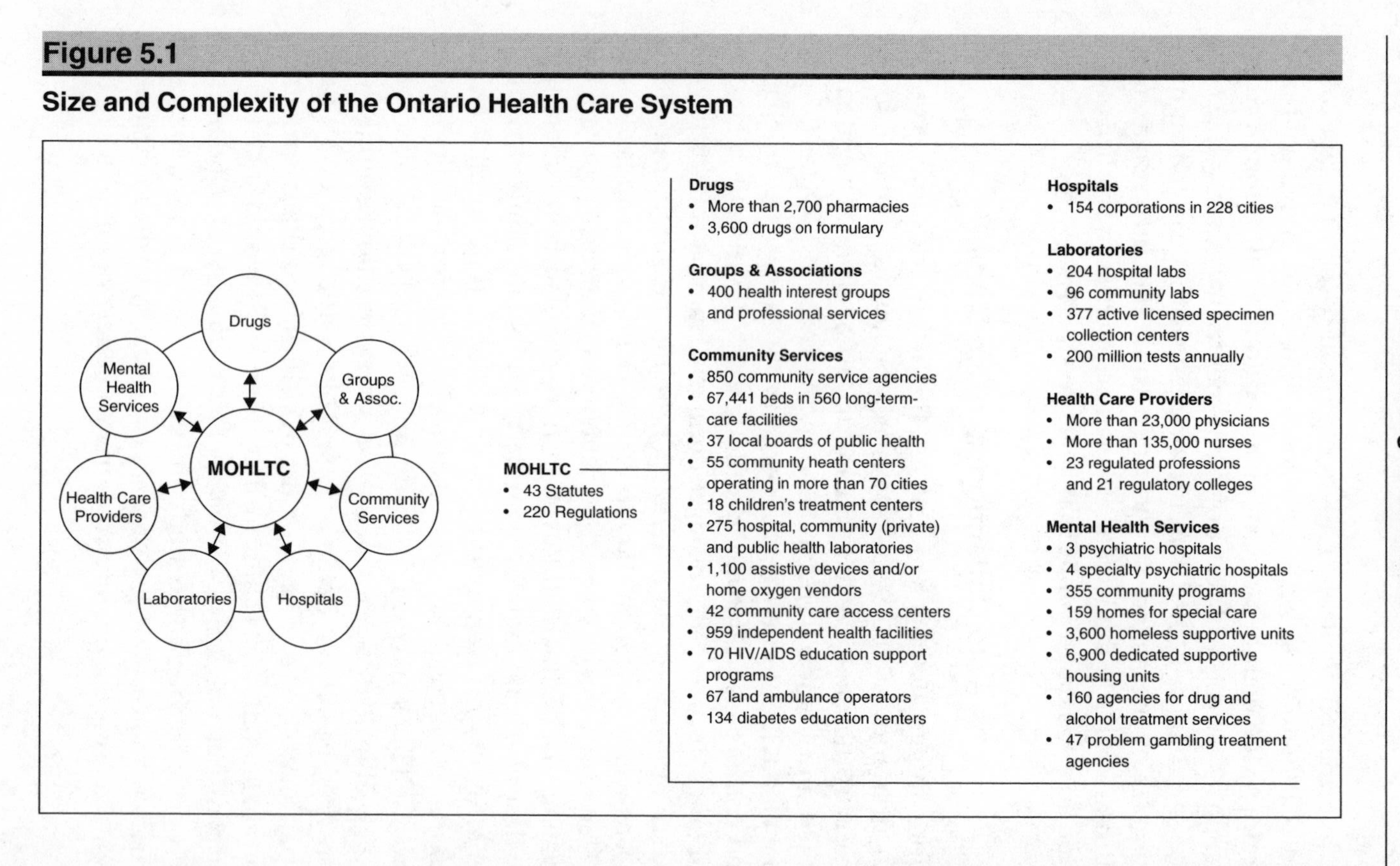

educate and persuade elected officials on the merits of investing in improved department performance.

Public service organizations in general too often assume that the more performance data collected the better. That approach is typically driven, as we have noted, by a performance focus on inputs and outputs, rather than on outcomes. The reality is that more metrics are not always better. The volume of metrics tracked may be assumed to equate with a sophisticated approach to performance management. A more common result, however, is for stacks of performance reports to pile up and not be acted upon, because no one is doing the necessary analysis to gauge whether performance is improving or not.

The more information management systems are used to manage an organization's operations, the easier it is to get access to the data needed to conduct meaningful performance measurement. If performance metrics have not been entered into some version of a shared information technology (IT) system, however, as in the case of Ontario, the administrative team retrieving metrics will have to carry out much of the work manually. It is typical in the public sector for departments or divisions of agencies to have stand-alone IT systems or ones that only superficially interface with other related systems. Cumbersome data collection, integration and analysis processes may result in redundant metrics being tracked with no added value.

Brown and his team retained Accenture in March 2005 to apply the Public Service Value methodology to the performance measurement data they had collected. As a first step, the Health Results Team and Accenture team confirmed the following outcomes and sub-outcomes, which we typically refer to as long-term and intermediate-term outcomes, with each sub-outcome supported by a handful of metrics that had been distilled from the health care system (see Figure 5.2).

Public sector entities that have invested in more sophisticated IT or business intelligence systems are more likely to have rela-

Figure 5.2

Ontario Health Care Public Service Value Outcome Model

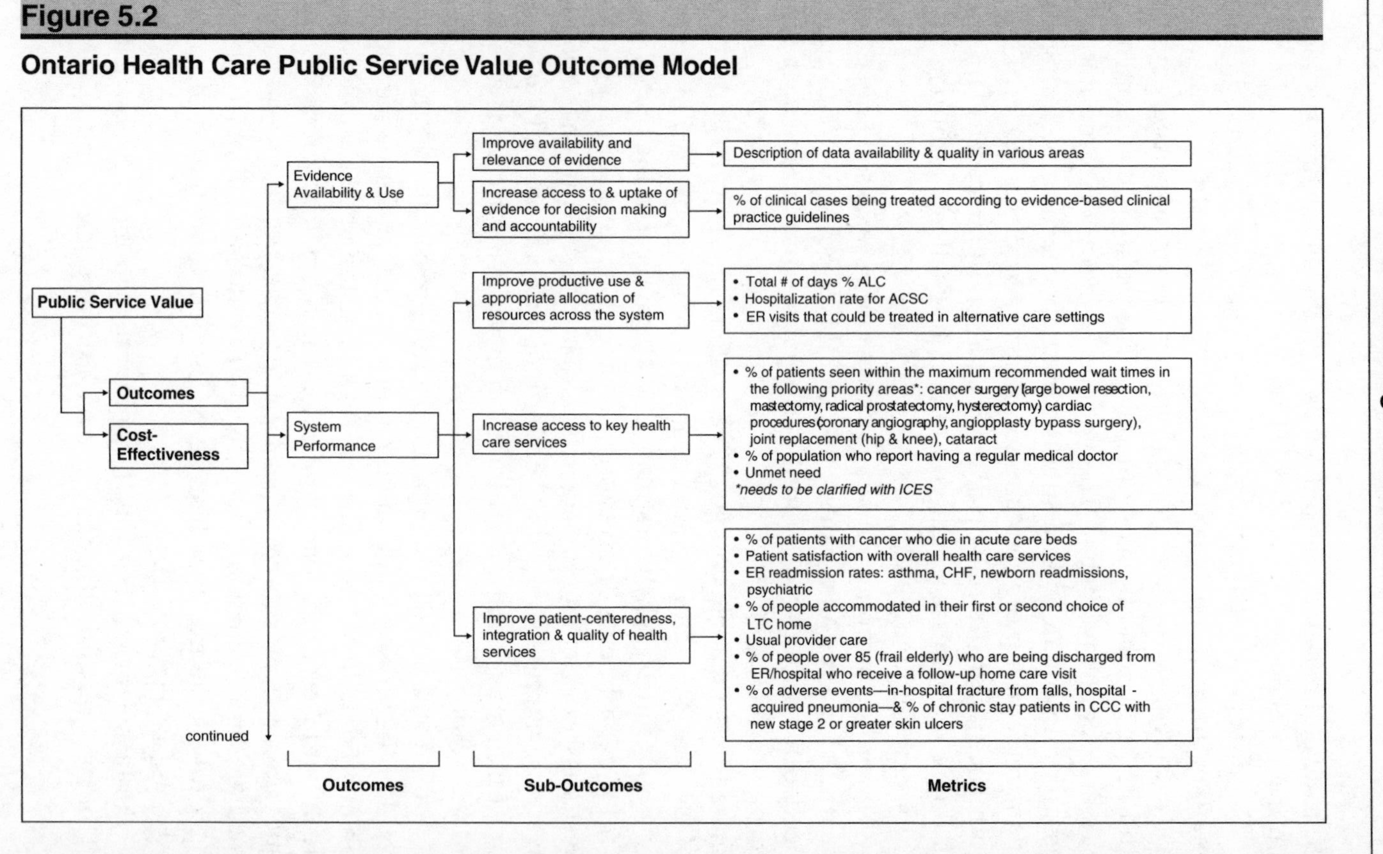

Figure 5.2

(continued)

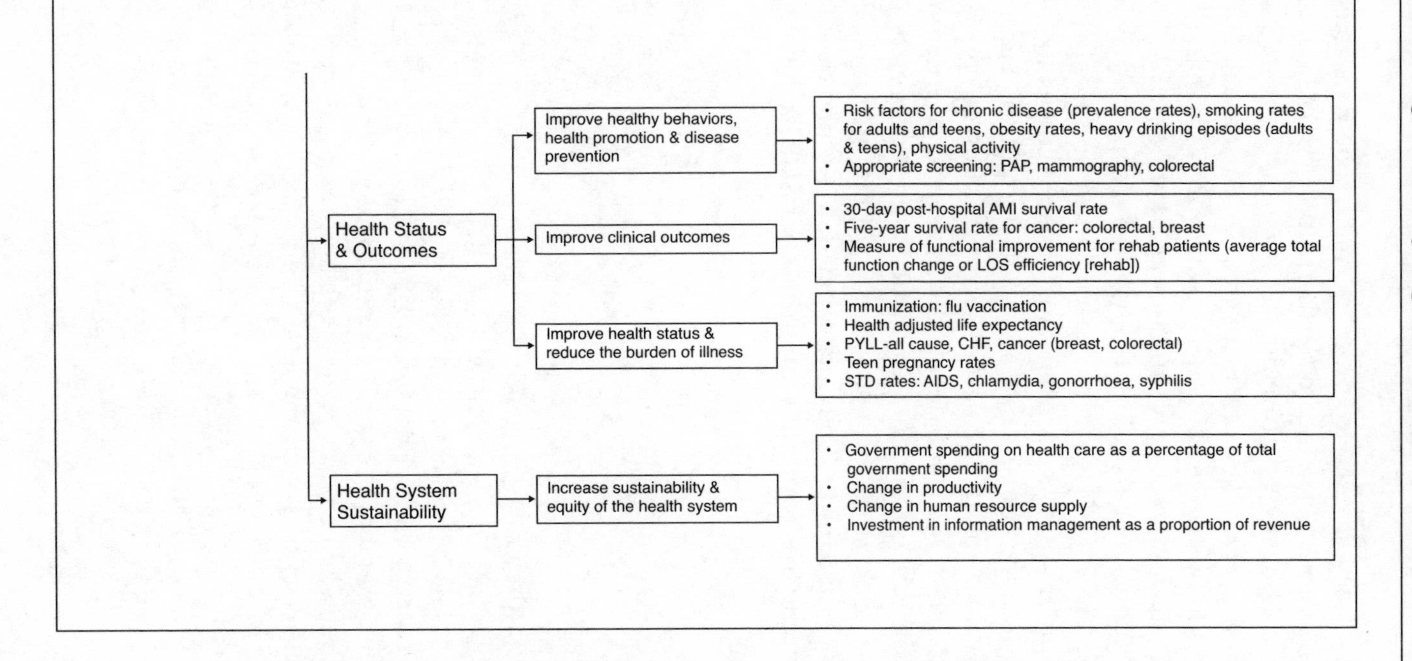

tively easy access to program data. For example, the Texas Medicaid and Healthcare Partnership (TMHP) had a highly integrated IT system that made accessing metrics relatively straightforward, recalled Accenture's Charles Sutton. He added that the state's IT system facilitated the team's ability to gather much more detailed data to support metrics and sub-metrics compared with the publicly available data that had been used in the 50-state Medicaid study. However, even the most up-to-date public service computer systems may fall short when it comes to collecting and analyzing customer service data. In part, this is because it is relatively rare for public service organizations to consistently track customer satisfaction levels. To understand whether taxpayers and other stakeholders are satisfied with the services they receive, public managers need to invest in finding out what their customers think or find reliable proxy data to substitute for customer service metrics and measures of public satisfaction.

A Different Approach

The Public Service Value methodology used in conjunction with the Ontario Health Care team is slightly different from our usual approach. First, it is unusual for the methodology to be applied to an entire health care system, as opposed to a particular public service organization. As we will discuss in a later chapter, however, we anticipate that future applications of our Public Service Value methodology are likely to encompass larger government systems. Secondly, this particular client engagement was unusual in that Accenture became involved in the performance measurement process at a relatively late date due to the fact that the client was thoroughly engaged in these activities as part of its mandate.

The Golden Rule

Ken Stark, director of the State of Washington's Division of Alcohol and Substance Abuse (DASA), is known for the sophisticated performance management and outcomes tracking system he has created. But Stark would be the first to concede that it has not been easy. In 1989, Stark and his team started with the concept that "there is no such thing as a free outcome. Measuring performance requires investment." He added, "You do not know whether you have achieved your results unless you know the baseline where you started." To that end they requested and received funding for what, in the early 1990s, was a state-of-the-art computer system with which to track DASA's ongoing performance. The latest iteration of the system, The Treatment and Report Generation Tool, or TARGET, has been online statewide since mid-2005.[2] Stark justifies funding requests with research from Washington, California and other states showing that every dollar invested up front in alcohol and substance abuse treatment and related spending saves taxpayers as much as seven dollars in future years that would otherwise be spent coping with the broadly defined social impact of untreated alcohol and substance abuse.

Stark's team mapped out a fairly comprehensive statewide management information system that today includes roughly 525 reporting agencies that provide services to DASA's clients. In the early years, in particular, Stark's team at DASA felt their share of political pressure from stakeholders, such as legislative staff and lobbyists, who tend to resist change and documentation of performance, Stark said. They countered this pressure by working to give as many stakeholders as possible a say in how the management system was configured. Stark also made agency compliance with the performance management system an integral part of providing DASA services. "We applied the Golden Rule," Stark said. "He with the gold rules." If agencies wanted to renew contracts and continue to receive DASA funding they had to buy into the performance management system and provide detailed measurement data and track whether they were meeting agreed-to outcomes. The results are impressive: Some 80 percent of DASA agencies participated in conducting a recent client satisfaction survey, which was filled out by 15,715 patients, or roughly 75 percent of the patients receiving services.

Tips to Gaining Allies for Analyses

- Involve legislative staff and other stakeholders up front in developing your performance measurement systems.
- Do not expect information to flow naturally when you want it. Give employees and organizations appropriate incentives to provide needed outcome data.

Running a Public Service Value Analysis

After tracking down the data needed to fill a Public Service Value outcome model, the next several steps in a Public Service Value analysis involve calculating the outcome and cost-effectiveness scores. These scores are essentially composites of all of the data used in the analysis. To calculate outcome and cost-effectiveness scores, basic statistical techniques are used to aggregate the performance data according to the assigned weights on the outcomes and metrics. To show the results of a Public Service Value analysis graphically, the outcome and cost-effectiveness scores are plotted on a two by two matrix. Outcome scores are represented on the vertical, or y-axis, while cost-effectiveness scores are plotted on the horizontal, or x-axis.

Adjusting Data: Standardization and Normalization

To calculate outcome and cost-effectiveness scores, however, raw data usually need to be adjusted. To do that, we employ two basic statistical techniques: standardization and normalization.

Standardization is a technique to compare data across multiple years. The most common form of data standardization is adjusting financial figures for inflation. By adjusting for inflation, it is possible to compare the price of a movie ticket in 1950 to a movie ticket today. Adjusting for inflation is a form of standardization that allows us to compare apples to apples to truly see the changes in data over time.

Daily Reality of Policing in London

The sizeable police force serving the roughly 7,000 residents of the City of London might at first blush be the envy of similarly sized towns across the United Kingdom. Why should the city deserve so many more officers per resident than the average British hamlet? The answer to that question highlights the need for data standardization. While it is true that only 7,000 people call the city home, an average of 350,000 commuters surge in and out of the historic urban center every workday. The city sets policing levels based on this total, if largely transitory, population as opposed to just permanent residents. To compare how effectively the City of London Police deliver law enforcement and public safety outcomes relative to other police forces, data for the force need to be standardized according to the total population of about 357,000.

Normalization is a technique to combine metrics with different base units such as the number of patients receiving a medical procedure and the amount of money spent on the procedure. Normalization converts raw data into a ratio that can then be combined with other data. To calculate an outcome score that combines metrics such as the number of welfare recipients served and the cost of serving a welfare recipient, we need to be able to combine two different base units: people and money. To normalize data, we divide a data point by a fixed value that is the average value of the base data set. The resulting ratio for each data point is a percentage above or below the average in the data set. Normalized data (percentages above or below the average) can then be added up to come up with a total outcome score:

Normalized score = Data point/Average of all data points across data set

Breaking Down Individual Outcomes

It is possible to make a detailed analysis of each outcome so that organizations may consider the relative, year-on-year change in the performance of one outcome compared with others. This type of analysis highlights the relationships between outcomes or initiatives taken in an attempt to improve performance. Public managers also are able to pinpoint specific areas of low or high performance for further examination.

As of late 2005, the Public Service Value analysis for Ontario's health care sector was still a work in progress, noted Brown. While he did not have final figures, he estimated that the early years of the current decade would reflect modest increases in outcomes at a relatively significant loss in cost-effectiveness. During these years there were significant infusions of cash into the health care system as hospitals were merged and changes were instituted in home and long-term care. Over the past two years (2004–2005) he expected to see outcomes and cost-effectiveness increase somewhat—moving toward the upper right-hand quadrant of the matrix—as the planned "investments" of the prior years actually began to bear fruit in terms of more positive health outcomes.

Introducing Cost-Effectiveness

The term *cost-effectiveness* means different things in different contexts. In the private sector, for example, it might mean return on sales (margin) or return on capital employed (ROCE), which is the ratio of net profits divided by the capital (invested funds, debt and equity) employed in generating that profit. Return on sales measures how much of each sale's value is eaten up by costs, while ROCE measures how well an organization uses its assets to generate profit. An important distinction between public managers and private sector managers is that public managers do not usually try to measure how well they use assets to generate profit. Instead they are interested in measuring the costs incurred to generate social return on taxpayers' money.

The Public Service Value methodology enables public managers to view cost-effectiveness in terms of the social return they are getting on their assets. The Public Service Value Model defines cost-effectiveness as the outcomes that an organization has achieved against the cost incurred, or the ratio of outcomes generated to the amount of resources consumed/employed in producing or delivering outcomes. Essentially, cost-effectiveness measures the social return on public investment.

Determining Cost-Effectiveness

When is an organization cost-effective? Why do we employ outcomes on both axes? Contrary to other models, the Public Service Value Model does not encourage public service organizations to unthoughtfully lower their cost bases as the easy way to improve value for money. By looking at cost-effectiveness as a ratio of outcomes produced to resources employed, the Public Service Value Model changes the focus from merely evaluating costs to evaluating costs vis-à-vis outcomes produced. This is an important distinction because a cost analysis would simply tell an organization which approach to service delivery is the most affordable. A cost-effectiveness analysis, on the other hand, yields a more important question: What is the highest social return for the level of resources employed?

Cost-effectiveness forces public managers to look beyond mere costs to the rate of change (increase or decrease) of costs compared to the rate of change in outcomes. For example, if outcomes increase at a faster rate than costs increase, or if costs are reduced at a faster rate than outcomes decrease, then cost-effectiveness goes up. However, if outcomes increase at a much slower pace than costs, or if outcomes decrease at a much faster pace than costs, then cost-effectiveness decreases. So cost-effectiveness, which is essentially a return on investment calculation, provides a "real" assessment of costs employed in delivering tangible benefits to taxpayers.

Balancing Capital and Revenue Expenditures

The verb "to invest" often seems to have a strange irregular form when used in a public service context: "I *invest* money in public services," "you *spend* money on public services," "they *waste* money on public services." Spending money in a way that can be claimed to be an investment is often taken to be "a good thing." So spending on new buildings for schools or hospitals, or much of the equipment that goes into them, is always brought forward by politicians as evidence of their commitment to a public service and, by inference, to the delivery of improved public value. But do these expenditures always create public value? Using a Public Service Value analysis, we can start to form a clear distinction between genuine "investment" in improving public value and just spending, or perhaps even wasting, public money.

Public Service Value analysis does this in the following way. First, any expense that can be classified as an investment is subtracted from annual operating expenditures to calculate cost-effectiveness. The cost of the investment is then amortized over the useful life of the investment and added back to the annual operating expenditures. The amount added back to annual operating expenditures is equal to the annual amortization of the investment plus a capital charge for the unamortized part of the investment calculated using the government borrowing rate. For the investment to produce a return of public value, the investment charges (amortization plus the capital charge) must be more than offset by increased outcomes delivered and/or reduced operating expenses.

Measured against this yardstick, many projects that are now unquestioningly seen as a good thing because they are presented as public "investments" will be reviewed in a different light. In this calculation, is a new school building the best way to improve educational outcomes and reduce the overall cost of education? Or might it be better to hire more or different kinds of teachers, to retrain existing teachers in new techniques, or perhaps restructure the school day? Could investment in a new general hospital lock us into current methods of health care delivery and inhibit the adoption of radical new methods of care in the future? More broadly, are we risking tying up large amounts of public money in inflexible capital stock that cannot be easily reallocated to meet changing approaches to raising outcomes cost-effectively and thus improving public value in the future?

If the goal is to improve public value, then it is not clear that spending money on a new project is necessarily a good thing until we understand the opportunity cost of other options for that same level of spending. When looking at proposed changes in expenditures, the key question is what impact they will have on public value.

This is not to say, however, that capital investment does not play a big part in improving public value. This is perhaps best illustrated by considering situations when budgetary cuts are required. In these situations it is very often capital expenditure that is cut when there is a choice between capital expenses and operating expenses. The reasons for this are obvious and to some extent unavoidable as politicians and officials seek to minimize the immediate impact of budgetary cuts on voters.

In the private sector in similar situations, similar considerations also come into play. The need to protect market share and profitability in the short term can dictate the curtailing of long-term investments. However, there are countervailing pressures. A company that was seen to be pumping up current profitability at the expense of necessary investment in future products and markets would likely see its stock price decline as the capital markets assessed short-term profitability against limited prospects for profitable growth in the future.

Public Service Value analysis helps weigh the balance between such fiscal pressures in the public sector and direct budget cuts to areas that need pruning in the short term to maintain or even enhance long-term prospects for future growth in public value.

How to Calculate Cost-Effectiveness

In the Public Service Value methodology, we calculate cost-effectiveness by dividing "normalized" outcomes over the adjusted cost per user.

Adjusted cost per user = Total costs × (operating expenditures + capital charge [adjusted for inflation]) divided by the target population

As this formula suggests, total cost includes both an organization's annual budget and its annual asset base.

The annual operating expenditure component can easily be found in the financial documentation that most public service organizations report annually. The annual operating expenditure is the day-to-day expenses incurred in running the organization, such as utilities, office supplies, salaries, bonuses, contract labor, insurance, postage, repairs, administrative, marketing, research and development, travel, training, depreciation and amortization, short-term projects and other expenses not exceeding one year.

The concept of a capital charge on the organization's asset base comes from the notion of opportunity cost. If a public service organization is holding assets, it is holding onto resources that could hypothetically be used for other public services. The return that a public service organization could get from these assets, if the organization did not hold them, can be approximated to the government bond or borrowing rate. We subtract current liabilities from the equation because total assets minus current liabilities is the true level of capital or net assets employed by the organization. Current liabilities are funds that are being used to operate the business on a daily basis, but not the funds that are used to help the organization achieve its outcomes.

Financial Adjustments Required to Calculate Cost-Effectiveness

1. *Calculating the Capital Charge.* The weighted average cost of capital is the standard methodology for considering the cost of holding assets within the private sector. Shareholders and debt holders expect a certain level of return on their investment. Their expectations are driven largely by the perceived risk of the company in which they are investing. Within a country, for example, the United Kingdom, the cost of debt in the public sector is consistent across government bodies because it is borne centrally by Her Majesty's

Treasury. Given this cost of debt, the prevailing 10-year government bond rate can be used to calculate the capital charge. Multiplying the total assets of the organization, less current liabilities, by this rate will provide an estimate of the capital charge, or the government's cost of holding assets.

2. *Determining Inflation Rates.* In our cost-effectiveness calculations, we discount total costs by the compounded rate of inflation. Depending on the country and the organization's sensitivity around the topic, the level of complexity required in calculating inflation can vary considerably. For instance, for a health organization, determining the inflation index may require a study of changes in prices for prescription drugs, health insurance, primary care services, surgical treatments, long-term care assistance, changes in human capital supplies (i.e. nurses and doctors) and so forth. The compounded inflation rate of all of these variables will produce a real rate of inflation for that specific industry.[3]
3. *Converting Cash Accounting to Accrual Accounting.* The accounting principles used by an organization affect the way expenses are reported in their financial statements. Organizations using accrual-based accounting assume that income is recognized or accrued as it is earned (regardless of when the money is received) and expenses are reported when they are incurred (regardless of whether they are paid or not). If an organization follows an accruals-based accounting system, there is no need for adjustments because income and expenses relate to the same years in which the outcomes were achieved.

   However, if an organization uses a cash-based accounting system, it records income when cash is received and expenses when they are paid. As a result, it fails to recognize the true value of the assets purchased because it records all expenses and investments as charges against the annual budget in the year that the expense is incurred (thereby failing to recognize a useful life greater than one year). If an organization uses cash accounting, it is necessary to make several accounting reconciliations to match the money spent on these assets with the years in which the benefits from that expense occur. Therefore, we need to adjust cash accounting figures to reflect accrual accounting's matching principle.

4. *Accounting for Off Balance Sheet Activity.* Public service organizations are increasingly recording off balance sheet activity. Given the nature of the information contained within the financial statements of government bodies, we need to consider whether adjustments should be made to these figures in order to provide a realistic assessment of cost-effectiveness.

   Specific areas where adjustments might be required to determine the most "fair" level of resources consumed by a government body include operating leases, unfunded pensions and private finance initiatives. For example, when an operating lease is material to the organization's overall expenditure and the cost of the lease plus the length of the lease is known, the lease should be capitalized onto the balance sheet. For this, we calculate the net present value by discounting future cash flows according to the organization's cost of capital. Then, we depreciate the asset over the life of the operating lease and add back that expense to the income statement. Finally, we calculate the capital charge on the operating lease by subtracting the value of the asset of net present value of future cash flows to the prior year accumulated depreciation.

Displaying Public Service Value Results

The Public Service Value performance matrix in Figure 5.3 represents graphically how an organization performed in the years covered by the analysis in terms of delivering both outcomes and cost-effectiveness. The matrix also highlights the concept of the average performance year. That is, each year is plotted on both axes as the deviation from the average performance score of outcomes and cost-effectiveness for the period of the analysis. The average performance is a score of "1" for both outcomes and cost-effectiveness.

The Public Service Value performance matrix plots *relative* rather than absolute scores. As such, the scores may be used to identify performance trends and changes, and to compare any one year's performance with average performance over time. Note that the Public Service Value performance matrix does not set out a mathematical relationship between x (cost-effectiveness deviation) and y (outcome deviation), nor does it intend to. It merely plots the two measures of performance alongside each other as an indication of relative performance. Like the outcome and metric filter processes, this scoring process is intended to provoke more insightful thinking and deliberation that will lead to actions focused on improved performance.

The Public Service Value performance matrix creates a baseline for comparing the performance of a public service organization by examining relative change over time. It does not indicate whether an organization on its own is performing well or poorly in absolute terms. Other kinds of traditional performance measures and comparisons of one organization's performance against other peer organizations are required for such absolute comparisons. Instead, the performance matrix demonstrates if an organization is performing better or worse than it did the year before.

On its own, the performance matrix does not tell the whole story. But, if a public service manager familiar with the history

Figure 5.3

Public Service Value Performance Matrix

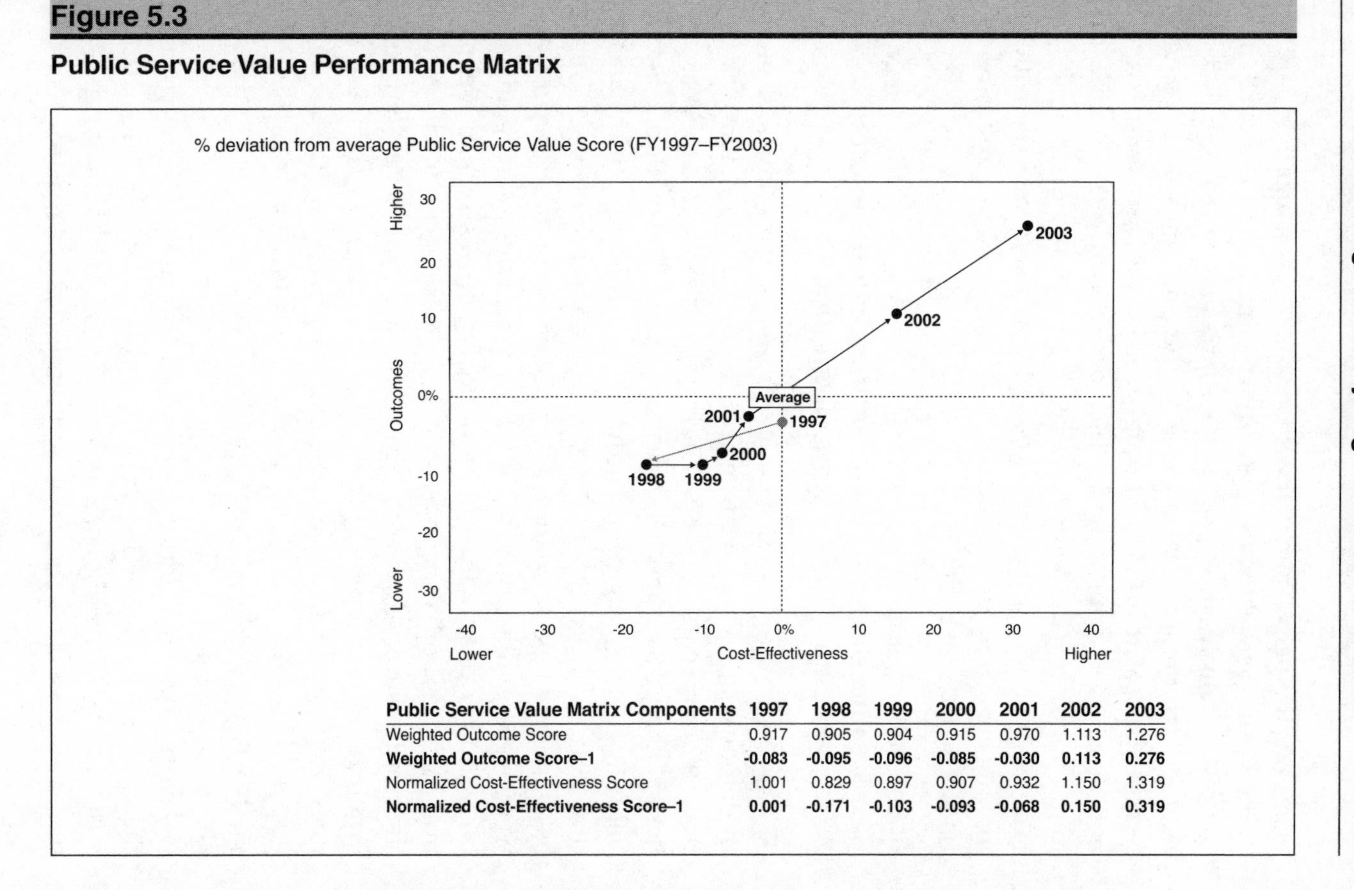

Public Service Value Matrix Components	1997	1998	1999	2000	2001	2002	2003
Weighted Outcome Score	0.917	0.905	0.904	0.915	0.970	1.113	1.276
Weighted Outcome Score–1	**-0.083**	**-0.095**	**-0.096**	**-0.085**	**-0.030**	**0.113**	**0.276**
Normalized Cost-Effectiveness Score	1.001	0.829	0.897	0.907	0.932	1.150	1.319
Normalized Cost-Effectiveness Score–1	**0.001**	**-0.171**	**-0.103**	**-0.093**	**-0.068**	**0.150**	**0.319**

examines the performance trajectory for the organization depicted in the Public Service Value performance matrix in Figure 5.3, he or she could identify the strategic decisions that were taken that may have contributed to the increase in the outcomes and cost-effectiveness scores from 2001 through 2003. Likewise, the decline in both cost-effectiveness and outcomes between 1997 and 1998 might highlight the negative, albeit temporary, impact of steps taken to prepare for the subsequent performance recovery, such as making up-front investments in staff, facilities or programs that take time to bear fruit.

Interpreting Public Service Value Results: The Value Compass

The strength of the Public Service Value methodology is its ability to demonstrate whether an organization is doing better or worse than in other years, and whether its performance in a given year is better than its average performance over time. The Public Service Value "compass" image in Figure 5.4 is a guide that translates the direction on the graph that an organization might move into an assessment of performance. A combination of north-south, east-west moves will identify whether the organization being analyzed is creating or destroying public value. For example, if an organization increases both outcomes and cost-effectiveness, it will move in the northeasterly direction, clearly creating value. As long as an organization continues moving north, increasing outcomes, and does not move west (decreasing cost-effectiveness), it is also creating public value. Likewise, if an organization moves due east (increasing cost-effectiveness) with no change in outcomes, it is also creating value.

The "ambiguous" indicators of value, denoted by gray circles on the compass in Figure 5.4, deserve special attention. These arrows indicate where the big challenge comes for public managers—and the ambiguity. To avoid falling into these gray areas for too long,

Figure 5.4

Public Service Value Compass

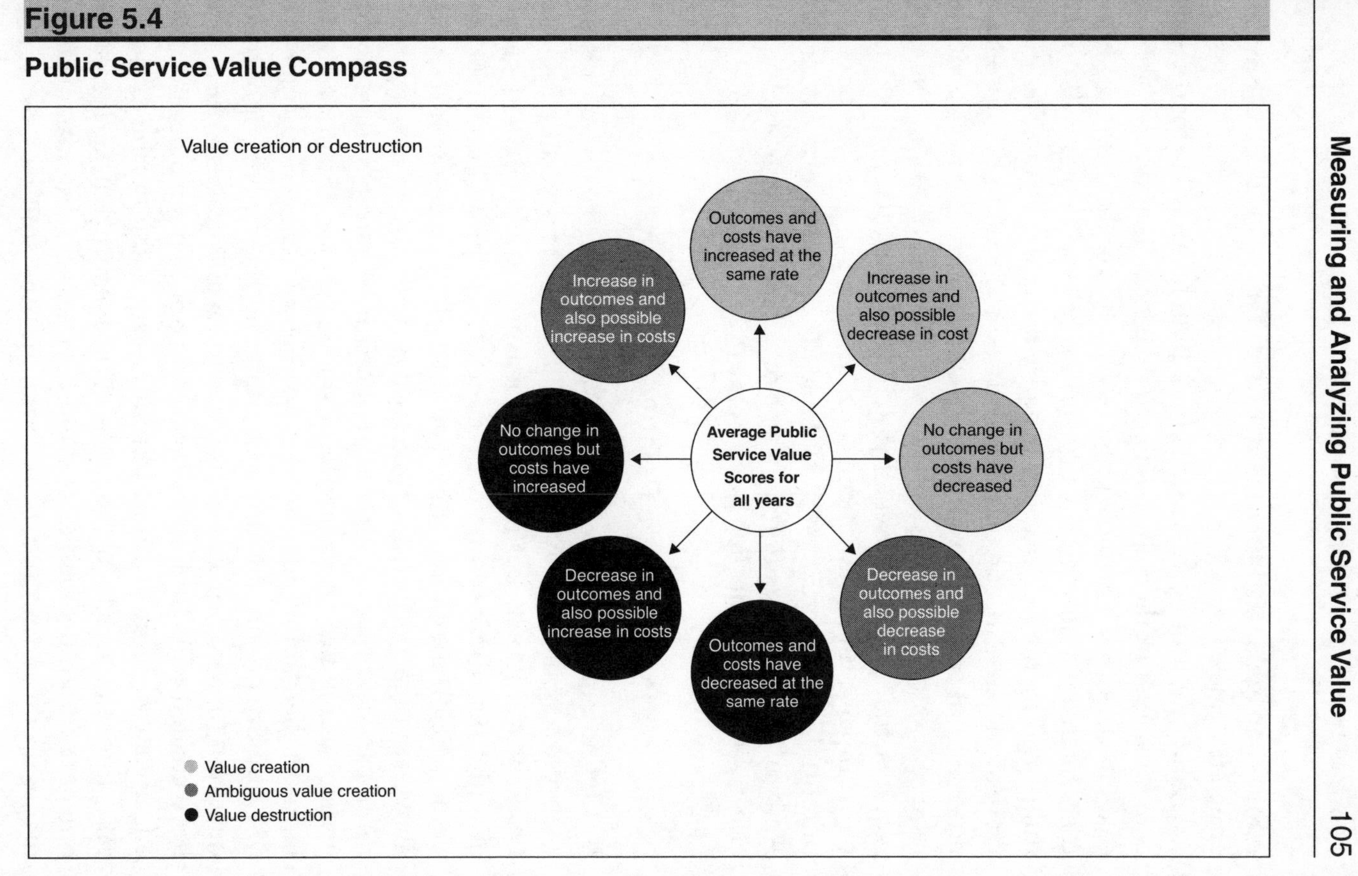

public managers need to think ahead and map out their value-creating strategies.

Frequently, public managers find that in order to boost outcomes, at least initially, they have to take steps that directly reduce cost-effectiveness. The most obvious example is absorbing up-front costs to create a new product or service or system that will not be fully implemented or reaping benefits for a few years. The initial modest increase in outcomes in such cases tends to be more than offset by decreased cost-effectiveness due to higher spending required. But that is not necessarily the wrong decision. Planning requires that managers weigh longer-term results against short-term impacts and plan ahead so that they can explain how the potential short-term pain will lead to long-term benefits. Ambiguous value creation may also result from an increase in cost-effectiveness but a decline in outcomes.[4]

Performance Relative to the Average

By definition, the Public Service Value Model evaluates results each year against an average for all years being studied. Other types of traditional performance measures are needed to gauge absolute performance in any given year. Using the Public Service Value Model, therefore, organizations will have some years with above-average performance and some with below-average performance. The four quadrants depicted in Figure 5.5 illustrate in general terms the performance of public service organizations in terms of their ability to achieve outcomes and cost-effectiveness.

Value-driven organizations landing in the upper right-hand quadrant for a particular year relative to their average performance have created value in terms of increasing both outcomes and cost-effectiveness. If an organization moves from the northeast quadrant into the northwest quadrant, it means that it increased outcomes and decreased cost-effectiveness. If an organization moves from the northeast quadrant into the southeastern quad-

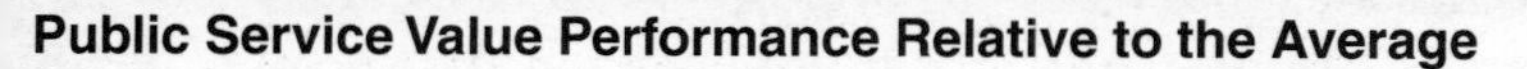

Figure 5.5

Public Service Value Performance Relative to the Average

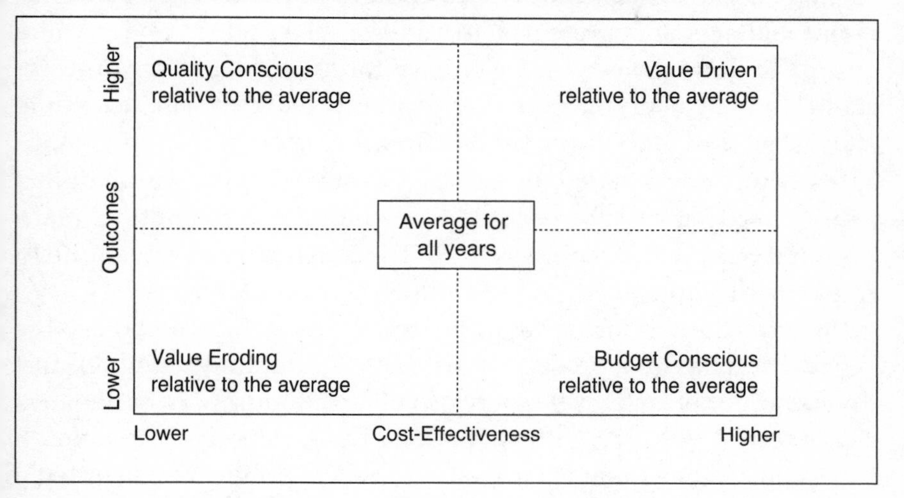

rant, it means that cost-cutting efforts are boosting cost-effectiveness, but at the expense of outcomes. And, if an organization moves from the northeast quadrant into the southwest quadrant, it is underperforming on all dimensions and has room to think creatively and strategically about how to turn its performance around.

Benefits and Limitations

As with any approach to performance measurement, the Public Service Value Model has a number of benefits and limitations. In terms of benefits, the principal one is that the measured focus on outcomes can help public managers better understand the connections between organizational purpose and action and make better informed decisions. The methodology provides for a sharper focus on the citizen stakeholder and monitors how efficiently taxpayer money is spent. In addition, by looking at the results of a public service organization holistically, trade-offs made between important outcomes and the cost of achieving outcomes can be analyzed. To this end, analyses can be used to determine the success of different management strategies. In addition, the Public Service Value approach shifts the debate away from target setting toward understanding of how public managers can improve performance while allocating scarce taxpayer money. In our experience, public managers who do not engage in a consideration of public value in this explicit manner can too easily default into the conventional management of inputs, processes and outputs, which may have little to contribute to improved public value in the longer term.

Of course, there are limitations to our model. It is contestable because it relies on a process of distilling a potentially complex and diverse set of objectives into a relatively small number of outcomes and metrics. Its weighting processes are largely judgmental, though we believe that is necessary to reflect political and strategic priorities. And comparisons across organizations are limited to those that deliver the exact same outcomes for very similar demographic groups, and we acknowledge that there are not very many of those that similar. Its main value is in comparing performance within one organization over time.

Even with these limitations, however, the Public Service Value methodology has the potential to make an important contribution to the debate on public services and public service reform. Ultimately, analytical models such as Public Service Value must be assessed on the strength of their capacity to improve the delivery of public services.

It is one thing to derive interesting information in an analysis about a public service organization. It is much more valuable to do something with that information that can make a difference in the lives of citizens. The Public Service Value methodology offers public service organizations a framework for assessing performance. Moreover, as we will see in the next chapter, the Public Service Value methodology can arm public managers with the information they need to make more informed decisions about what can be done to meet important public needs. In this sense, the Public Service Value Model is a means to an end, not an end in itself. The end, or perhaps a new beginning, is for public managers to spend their scarce time using the information they gain to find ways to create even more value for the public.

Driving Results

After gathering performance information from Public Service Value analyses, the next question is how public managers can use the information to identify specific changes to make to improve performance and unlock public value. In this chapter, we look at international examples, including a German retirement pension insurance carrier, a U.S. Medicaid agency, a European intelligence agency and European labor agencies, to illustrate how performance information from Public Service Value analyses can be used to inform strategic decisions to drive better results and achieve high performance.

The administrators of one of Germany's largest regional retirement pension insurance carriers, Landesversicherungsanstalt (LVA) Hannover (in 2005 renamed Deutsche Rentenversicherung Hannover/Braunschweig), were not used to competition. After all, LVA Hannover's mission was to provide insurance coverage, offer medical rehabilitation and calculate and pay pensions for more than 900,000 retirees and 2 million insured persons. Providing this type of social services had been the responsibility of the German government since the latter part of the nineteenth century and formed the basis of Germany's modern welfare state.

In January 2005, however, all of that changed. Germany's Federal Insurance Institution for Employees and 22 state insurance institutions were merged to form the German Retirement Pension Insurance (Deutsche Rentenversicherung). As a result, LVA Hannover scrambled to slash costs and improve services to compete with the other German insurance agencies. To better understand its own strengths and weaknesses, LVA Hannover employed the Public Service Value methodology.

The Public Service Value analysis plotted six outcomes for the agency and 13 metrics to track how well LVA Hannover was attaining these outcomes (see Figure 6.1). The analysis indicated that

FIGURE 6.1

Landesversicherungsanstalt (LVA) Hannover Public Service Value Performance Matrix

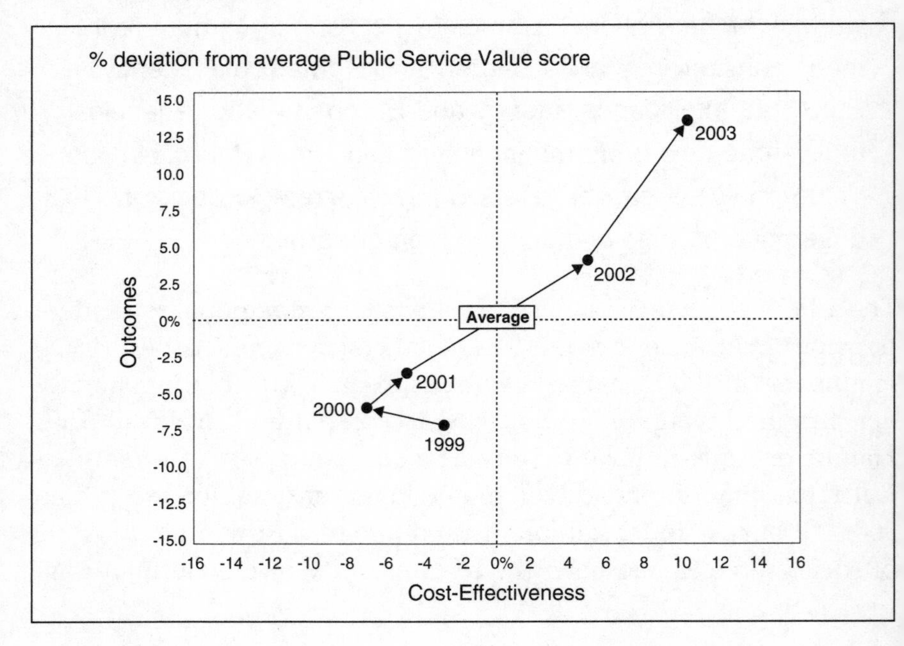

LVA Hannover had been creating value since 2000, with significant increases in both outcomes and cost-effectiveness between 2001 and 2003. The agency found that its strengths were in maximizing the fairness of contributions, optimizing rehabilitation to counter disabilities and offering more comprehensive and need-related consultation.

Even though the analysis showed significant improvements, it also identified a relative decline in the accuracy of payments of retirement pensions related to recent legislative changes. Therefore, one of the challenges identified for LVA Hannover was to react swiftly to future legislative changes through, for example, focused knowledge management and personnel training. The Public Service Value analysis showed that if it could advance in these specific areas, LVA Hannover could even further improve its performance.

As this example with LVA Hannover attests, using the Public Service Value approach can provide an organization with a fresh window to evaluate its performance. However, the results of a Public Service Value analysis alone cannot tell public managers exactly *why* its performance is trending in a certain direction. To understand the factors causing performance to change in one way or another, managers need to go one step further and investigate the value drivers or the actions the organization took and other external conditions that might have shifted performance.

Identifying Value Drivers

Value drivers tend to be specific to a certain policy arena such as education, health care or defense. In certain cases they may even be specific to a given strategy pursued by a particular organization within that policy area. Identifying value drivers allows an organization to focus scarce resources on the few precise actions that have the greatest likelihood of influencing performance results.

The Public Service Value methodology can be used to focus public managers' attention on those policies or choices that will have the greatest impact on their organizations' ability to achieve its intended outcomes, such as providing insurance coverage or medical rehabilitation for Germans. Typically, the managers in an organization have good information about what actions will produce what results and should always be consulted to gain an in-depth understanding of value drivers. If managers are able to identify the specific actions that contributed to more Germans getting access to insurance, for example, then they can use those value drivers in the future to evaluate the pros and cons of new policy changes. When using value drivers to make new decisions, however, it is critical to consider timing and context to make sure that what worked the first time will have similar results in today's environment.

Any analysis that moves the debate on from whether an outcome has been met toward a better understanding of how managers can use this information to create better outcomes more cost-effectively is of great potential benefit. The Public Service Value approach is designed to help achieve this advance by identifying those drivers that have the greatest impact on public sector performance.

CompStat Credo

Many U.S. police departments struggled in the 1980s and early 1990s with measuring the effectiveness of law enforcement—focusing on measuring outputs such as the number of officers on the beat rather than on outcomes such as reductions in crime. Then came CompStat, which has dramatically changed the focus of performance measurement in police departments in the cities where it has been applied.

CompStat started in 1994 when New York City realized that the police were measuring and trumpeting to the media the number of arrests, and other related outputs, when what taxpayers really wanted was a straightforward outcome: less crime. Under the leadership of then Police Commissioner William Bratton and Deputy Commissioner Jack Maple, the NYC police department began holding weekly, then twice-weekly, crime control strategy meetings focused on computerized crime and related statistics (hence the name CompStat) from each of the city's 77 precincts.

CompStat meetings cut through the rigid hierarchy of rank within the police force to bring together officers of all ranks to "draw upon the department's collective expertise to develop new strategies and tactics," said *The Price of Government* co-authors Osborne and Hutchinson.[1] The CompStat approach gave precinct commanders authority, and responsibility, for all aspects of police work in their area. In addition, it gave them the ability to use current data on crime and the group's collective knowledge to determine what factors were driving the results so that they could focus efforts on increasing the ultimate outcome of public safety. Police brass made it clear that officers had to buy into the CompStat approach if they were to remain on the force. With the crime rate in New York City falling in nearly every major category for the balance of the decade, many credited CompStat with contributing to the noticeable decrease (along with demographic changes and other factors).

As word of New York's success spread, CompStat and similar approaches were adopted by police forces in Los Angeles (where Bratton currently serves as commissioner), Chicago, Washington, D.C., Baltimore, and several other major cities, and were considered successes. In addition, Baltimore and other cities, including Chattanooga, Syracuse and Anchorage, began applying CompStat to other city functions. Baltimore in

2000 coined the name CitiStat (and hired Jack Maple as a consultant) to convey the way in which the accountability performance measurement system was being adopted citywide to improve performance—from garbage collection to transportation. Initial results showed impressive gains in departmental performance, and multi-million dollar costs savings from sharp drops in absenteeism and overtime.[2]

Balancing Trade-offs to Maximize Public Service Value

In considering the value drivers of high performance, it is also critical to remember that sometimes an action taken to improve performance in one outcome can have unintended consequences and actually lead to a decrease in another outcome. For instance, if a revenue agency focuses more resources on collecting taxes and expanding their audit department, the outcomes of maximizing revenue and compliance rates should increase. However, if many audits do not yield fruit and the agency is perceived as being more aggressive and less customer friendly, the outcome of customer satisfaction may decrease. If the action is perceived as creating more equitable enforcement, however, customer satisfaction might rebound. In such instances, public managers can use the Public Service Value methodology as a framework to evaluate trade-offs between outcomes and the spending required to achieve them.

Strategies to maximize public value should take into consideration all of an organization's outcomes. Focusing on one particular outcome at the expense of the others might reap rewards in one outcome area in the short term, but will rarely deliver long-term value overall. At some point, prolonged focus on a particular outcome may yield diminishing returns. In an extreme case, overemphasis on a particular outcome might also see other outcomes start to slip as management attention wanders from them. It is no good worrying only about one or two outcomes when there are three or four to be achieved.

A management strategy aimed at maximizing public value will therefore look at all outcomes carefully. It will tend to favor incremental improvement in a number of outcomes rather than an extreme focus on any one outcome alone. A value-maximizing strategy is sensitive to the trade-offs between statutory outcomes, or outcomes stated in the mission or statutory purpose of an organization, and delivery outcomes, or outcomes related to service delivery levels. When there is a specific need, perhaps because of political or electoral pressure, to focus on improving one outcome over another, a public manager should remain alert to the impact that this focus may have on other outcomes and seek to mitigate the effects. A change in the delivery of service might also improve statutory outcomes. For example, a focus on delivering efficient customer service (a delivery outcome) in a revenue agency might also improve compliance and tax yield (statutory outcomes).

Outcomes Drive Strategic Planning

In 2005, the Texas Medicaid and Healthcare Partnership (TMHP) used the Public Service Value outcome framework it developed to facilitate its long-term planning process. The TMHP team took the Public Service Value analysis to a leadership retreat in February 2005. Kate Brodsky, Project Management Specialist for Operations at TMHP, explained how, during the retreat, leaders from TMHP and the state Health and Human Services Commission (HHSC) reviewed their four outcomes and decided to use them as the basis for identifying ways to make strategic improvements to the Medicaid Program. After reviewing each of the four outcomes, they developed initiatives that would lead TMHP to achieve the outcomes.

Following the retreat, TMHP created the 2006 Annual Business Plan, which is the group's road map for the fiscal year (see Figure

6.2). It is developed each year by TMHP with added input from HHSC. The plan was developed as a management as well as a measurement tool to allow TMHP to "clarify our vision and mission and translate them both into action," said Brodsky. With the Public Service Value outcomes as the umbrella structure, the Annual Business Plan contains specific goals, approaches and initiatives that TMHP can use throughout the fiscal year to improve the Medicaid Program.

The TMHP Annual Business Plan ties strategies and goals to concrete initiatives aimed at enhancing public value. The chart in Figure 6.3 traces how one of five goals links approaches and initiatives to add value.

The TMHP example shows how the Public Service Value methodology can help an individual agency find ways to improve performance. But, it can also be used to uncover insights across an entire policy area in a region or even in a country. At these larger geographical levels, the Public Service Value approach can enable comparison of the performance results of multiple organizations. Of course, as stated earlier, this only works well when service delivery is similar and when the external factors that may skew results (macroeconomic conditions, demographics and even the politics) are similar across the group of organizations. So, for example, comparing implementation of a federal program across a number of similar states can provide useful comparative information and foster learning across agencies.

Intelligence Test

Intelligence agencies may not be the first governmental bodies to come to mind when one thinks of the need, or desire, to drive performance by boosting cost-effectiveness and outcomes, but they feel budgetary constraints just like most other public service organizations. Recently, some European intelligence agencies found value in applying a combination of Public Service Value and

Figure 6.2

Texas Medicaid & Healthcare Partnership 2006 Annual Business Plan

Strategy: Minimize Administrative Burden

Goal: Process all transactions accurately and efficiently
Approach:
- Promote quality through continuous improvement
- Reduce use of paper
- Ensure claims adjudication procedures are aligned with policy

Goal: Empower providers through use of the Internet
Approach:
- Enhance portal functionality
- Increase provider knowledge

Strategy: Maximize Access

Goal: Improve healthcare while reducing costs
Approach:
- Become actively involved in improving health outcomes
- Propose and implement cost containment initiatives

Goal: Empower providers through use of the internet
Approach:
- Enhance portal functionality
- Increase provider knowledge

Goal: Project a positive image
Approach:
- Increase public knowledge of management and delivery of healthcare services

Strategy: Optimize Revenue and Medical Costs

Goal: Process all transactions accurately and efficiently
Approach:
- Promote quality through continuous improvement
- Reduce use of paper
- Ensure claims adjudication procedures are aligned with policy

Goal: Improve healthcare while reducing costs
Approach:
- Become actively involved in improving health outcomes
- Propose and implement cost containment initiatives

Goal: Maintain a collaborative and rewarding workplace
Approach:
- Improve team member satisfaction
- Improve cross-organizational decision-making

Strategy: Maximize Utilization of Preventive Services

Goal: Improve healthcare while reducing costs
Approach:
- Become actively involved in improving health outcomes
- Propose and implement cost containment initiatives

Figure 6.3

Texas Medicaid & Healthcare Partnership

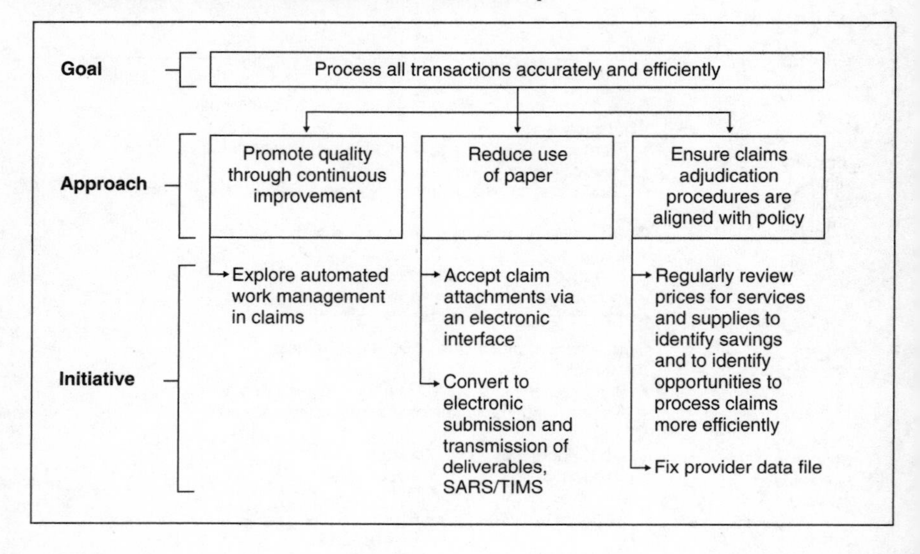

Balanced Scorecard methodologies to meet their daunting challenge of balancing critical mission goals with a call for more efficient operations.

Each year the agencies have to "raise the bar" on achieving their mission-critical outcomes (such as penetrating international terrorist organizations). Although each intelligence agency differs in its specific mission, all of the agencies share similar back office support and administration capabilities. With a common set of Public Service Value measures covering the areas where their operations overlapped, the agencies were able to employ a new way of tracking operational performance and comparing performance improvement rates across their common "back office" functions. Although overall performance may be difficult to compare across intelligence agencies with different missions, it was possible to compare performance in key functional areas. In addition, the cost-effectiveness dimension of the Public Service Value framework gave the agencies a way to identify process efficiencies by sharing best practice, rather than reverting simply to across-the-board cost reductions or automation of labor-intensive processes.

The Public Service Value approach also built on the agencies' previous investment in Balanced Scorecard techniques. The two performance management frameworks proved to be compatible since both look for ways to balance performance goals across multiple dimensions. The Balanced Scorecard identifies metrics along four dimensions—financial, customer, process and people—and seeks to balance the pursuit of targets across all four. Combining both techniques offered the agencies a way to measure financial performance by evaluating cost-effectiveness, customer performance by evaluating delivery of outcomes and process and people performance by evaluating the agencies' development of core capabilities. Linking outcome and cost-effectiveness measurement to capabilities was attractive because many of the agencies' capabilities are so unique that they are hard to compare externally.

The agencies appreciated that linking capabilities to outcomes and cost-effectiveness could be used to both design a "to be" target state and examine the "as is" situation in order to then assess gaps and identify the business changes required to meet future targets. These agencies typically operate on a five-year planning cycle and thus need to predict what future capabilities they will need to secure investment funding from the government. The agencies liked this combined approach and saw immediate benefit in comparing the performance of similar core capabilities across agencies to help identify best practices in the intelligence community and thus improve the performance of all agencies. Linking outcomes to financial results gave the agencies the financial discipline necessary to drive cost-effective investment in the core capabilities to improve performance. Indeed, many within the agencies commented that measuring results with business cases prevented overinvestment in "Rolls Royce" solutions or underinvestment.

Valuing Labor

In 2006, a Public Service Value study was released that compared performance results of labor agencies from various countries including Germany, the United Kingdom and the Netherlands. The study covered the years 1997 through 2004, and demonstrated the benefit of using citizen-based outcomes to measure performance.[3] The outcome model used in the study reflected the controllable set of outcomes across labor agencies as opposed to the political outcomes that would vary by country. The labor study is a powerful example of how the Public Service Value Model can be used to compare, evaluate and learn from the performance of organizations in a particular policy area.

The underlying Public Service Value labor outcome model reflects the services provided by most of the labor agencies, including services such as job matching, training and benefits administration. Some of the countries studied divide these same services among multiple agencies. To cover the entire spectrum of services in such cases, the analysis needed to be extended to all agencies responsible for job matching, training and benefits in the national labor market.

The Public Service Value outcome model in Figure 6.4 was used as the underlying framework for the study.

In the study, each outcome and metric was assigned a weight. The weights were selected by labor experts from each country to reflect as close as possible the priorities that the group shares in their labor programs. Figure 6.5 is an example of the model applied to the first, and most heavily weighted, outcome—Maximize Job Matching Services—as well as its related metrics and sub-metrics.

The cost-effectiveness calculations included only those costs connected to the specific labor outcomes that were directly influenced by the agencies. The cost of core services set by law, such as unemployment benefits, were not included since the agencies did not directly control those costs.

In summary, the labor study revealed the different results of

Figure 6.4

Public Service Value European Labor Outcome Model

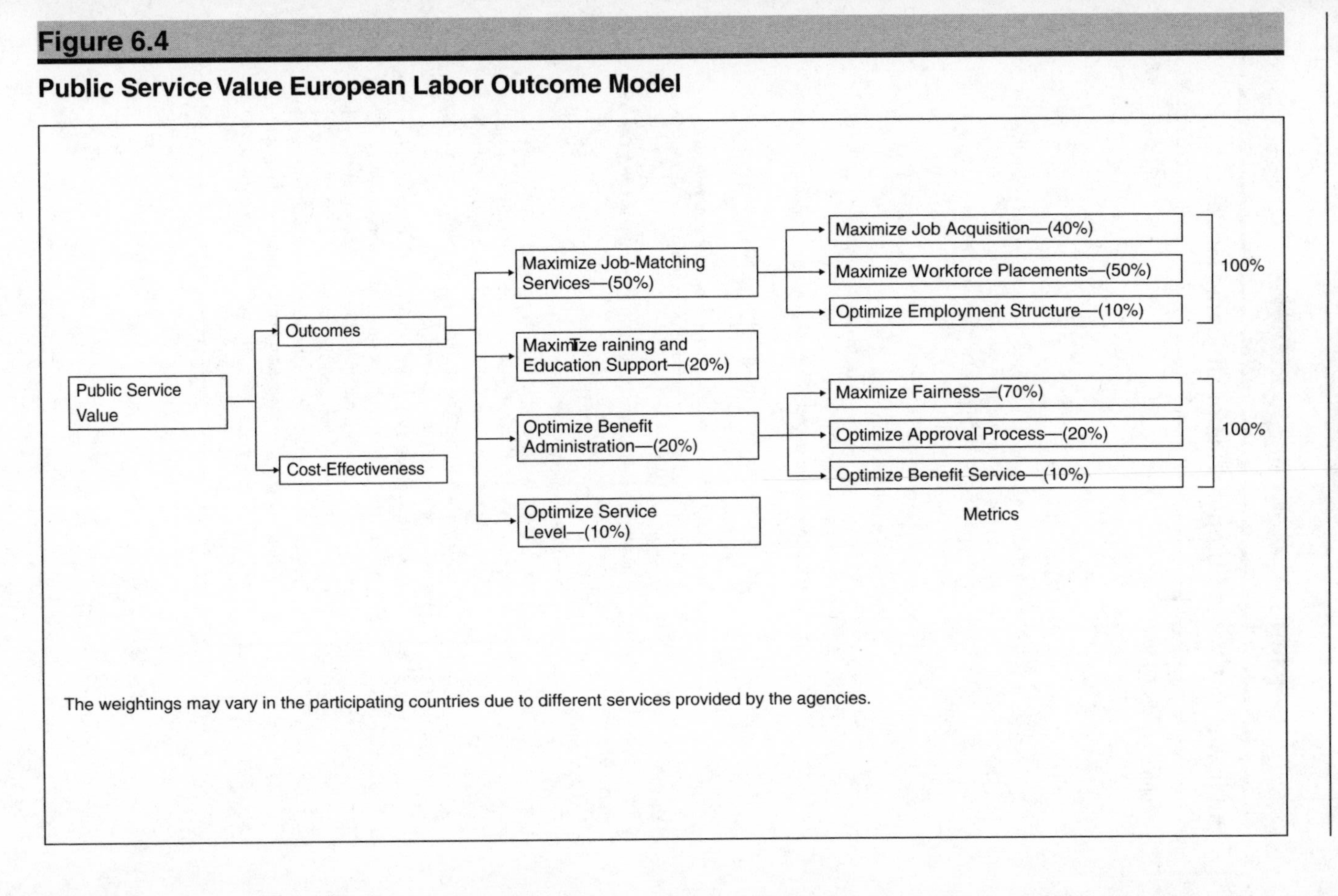

The weightings may vary in the participating countries due to different services provided by the agencies.

Figure 6.5

Public Service Value European Labor Outcome Model

Metrics and Sub-Metrics

Maximize Job Matching Services—50% (Outcome)

Maximize Job Acquisition—(40%)

- Percentage of vacancies registered by the agency over the total number of vacancies in the labor market
- Percentage of self-employed within supporting program over the number of unemployed

Maximize Workforce Placements—(50%)

- Duration of filling a job vacancy
- Percentage of placements by the agency over the number of incoming vacancies
- Percentage of placement offers over the number of placements by the agency
- Percentage placements using recruiting aids that have led to a non-aided recruitment
- Percentage of vacant positions for apprenticeship without a training position over the number of applicants for an apprenticeship training position
- Percentage of vacant positions filled with in agreed time frame by employer and agency

Optimize Employment Structure—(10%)

- (Percentage of placements of priority publics [youth, older woman, low qualified, long-term unemployed, single parents] by the agency over the number of incoming unemployed of priority publics) over (percentage of placement by the agency over the number of incoming unemployed)
- (Percentage of placed apprentices of priority publics by the agency over the number of incoming applicants of priority publics) over (percentage of placed apprentices by the agency over the number of incoming applicants)
- Percentage of placements by the agency valid for more than the probation period over the total number of placements by the agency (if probation period is not applicable, use reasonable time frame which, is measured in agencies)

each country's labor program. Based on those results, a deeper analysis uncovered the value drivers or specific actions that the organizations took to achieve those results. Those lessons can be shared among the labor organizations as they consider potential actions in the future.

Comparative Learning

Public service organizations in different states or countries sometimes try to benchmark themselves against similar organizations as a way of gauging their own success. However, because not all organizations operate in the same political and socio-economic environment, and because data reliability varies, it is difficult to find reliable comparable data sets across organizations in different geographies.

A 2005 Organization for Economic Cooperation and Development report titled "Modernizing Government: The Way Forward" cautions against making facile comparisons among different agencies in different countries.[4] Context is king. The report suggests that in order to make relevant comparisons between national governing systems, they should be placed on a continuum between each of the following areas:

- Collective versus individual human resource management
- Unified versus diverse national culture
- High versus low compliance risk
- Centralized versus delegated management
- High-prestige versus low-prestige public service
- Dominant *ex ante* versus *ex post* controls
- Strong versus weak parliamentary scrutiny
- Open versus secretive administrative cultures
- Unified versus distributed public agencies
- Strong versus weak unionization
- Cooperative versus confrontational industrial relations
- Career-based versus position-based public service systems

- High versus low tendency to use market-type mechanisms and private agents

Reviewing organization performance from different locations based on the above criteria will highlight similarities and differences, and dispel stereotyped views influenced by geographic proximity and historical ties. Relying on such stereotypes tends to underestimate differences within countries that are thought of in general terms as culturally similar. Based on the above framework, the report notes that, counterintuitively, "There may be more similarities between Japan and France than between, say, France and Italy."[5]

Notwithstanding the challenges in comparing organizations across different geographies, the Public Service Value methodology was applied to 50 state studies in the United States in select policy areas such as child support and Medicaid. These studies provide a unique view of performance and what is driving that performance for the organizations examined and a good basis for learning.

The Public Service Value study of child support agencies across all 50 U.S. states offered valuable insights into industry-wide trends. However, as noted in Chapter 3, the lack of consistently reliable data from many states provided challenges in interpreting the results. As a result, the study utilized nationwide summary data for the years 1993 through 2004. Figure 6.6 shows the measurement framework, with the outcomes, metrics and weights used to track value creation for U.S. child support agencies.

The study found that a significant increase in child support outcomes occurred in 1998 and was accompanied by a corollary increase in child support expenditures. Examining these results with U.S. child support experts yielded a hypothesis that the passage and implementation of the 1996 Personal Responsibility and Work Opportunity Reconciliation Act contributed to the noticeable rise in child support outcomes and expenditures. The 1996 Act established new requirements for state child support agencies and cre-

Figure 6.6
Public Service Value Child Support Enforcement Outcome Model

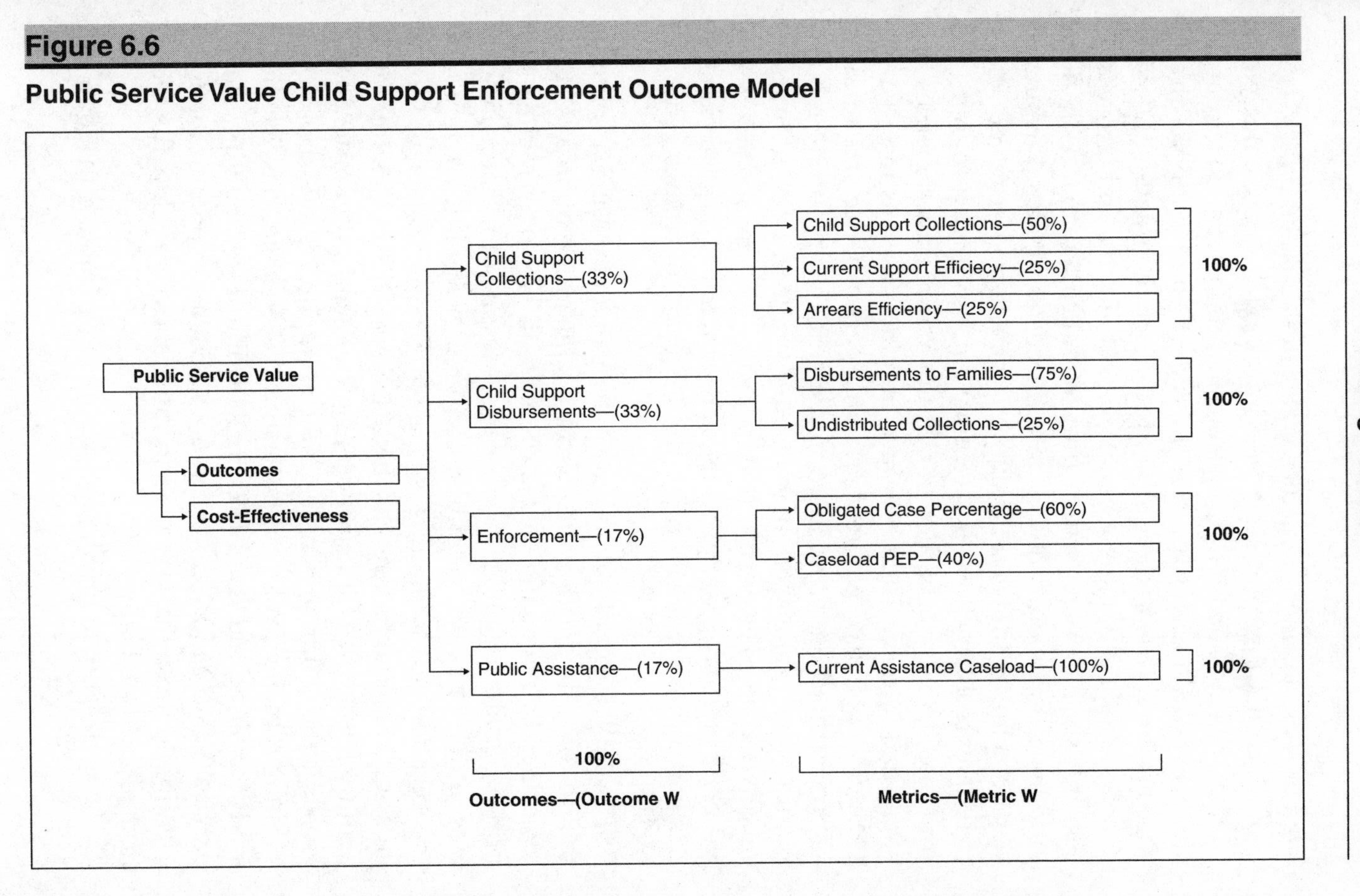

ated new enforcement remedies that states could employ to collect past due child support. Some examples of the new enforcement approaches included requiring states to automate and standardize the wage-withholding process to collect child support directly through payroll deductions. Prior to the Act, the wage-withholding process had been largely manual, with forms and procedures varying state to state, which proved difficult for large, national employers to follow. The Act introduced the financial institution data match that allows child support agencies to freeze and seize a delinquent obligor's bank account. An incentive program was introduced that established minimum performance metrics that states had to meet. Failure to meet minimum scores resulted in a financial penalty, whereas strong performance resulted in increased funding. In addition, more stringent reporting requirements were established that resulted in increased accuracy of reported data. The results indicate how an investment within the child support program to increase automated system capabilities had a direct impact on the child support outcomes generated by states.

The child support study shows the value of having a common tool to compare performance across a large group of organizations over time. By reviewing the results of 50 different states' child support programs together, it is possible—despite differences in agencies and states—to identify changes in public policy and organization spending that shaped the performance results. A cross-organization study can be a treasure trove of information about what levers child support agencies can pull in order to better serve the children, families and communities they serve.

Similar to the child support study, a 50-state U.S. Medicaid study, covering the years 1998 to 2001, illustrated how the Public Service Value Model can be used to compare organizations by identifying those that were performing above or below the industry average (see Figure 6.7).

The trick is not to use these comparisons to rank or to judge, but

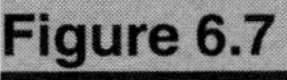

Figure 6.7

United States 50-State Public Service Value Medicaid Study

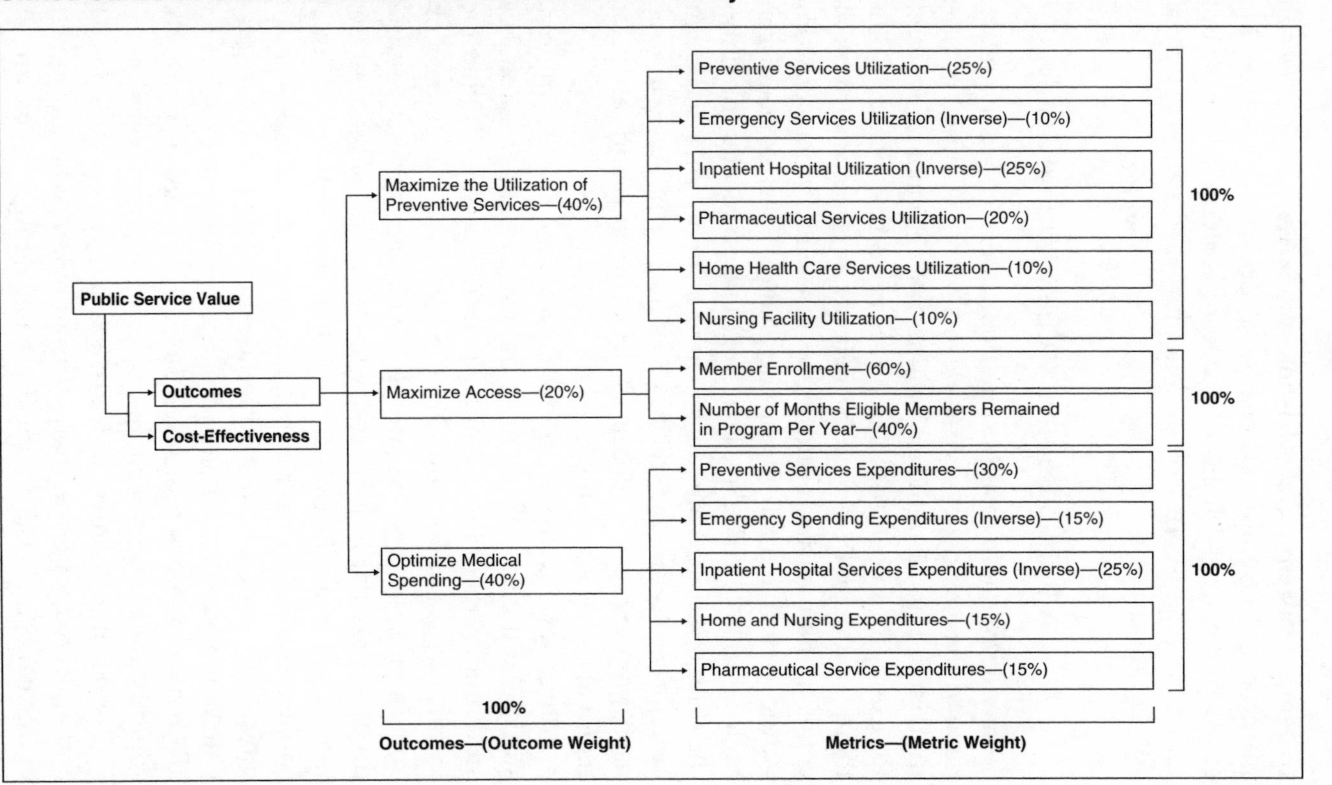

to learn from the comparisons about what might be done to increase public value. The adaptation of the 50-state Medicaid study to the Texas Medicaid Program is a good example of how to tailor the analysis of an outcome model to suit an organization's specific needs.

A Public Service Value National Study

It may be possible to apply the Public Service Value methodology beyond the agency level to achieve a more "whole of government" understanding of delivering value at a regional or national level, for example. To conduct a Public Service Value study of this type, there would first need to be general agreement around the outcomes to be measured and the weightings of those outcomes that would reflect overall goals and stakeholder expectations at the regional or country level. That might be politically contentious, but the Public Service Value technique for identifying and quantifying outcomes as discussed in Chapter 4 and in the Appendix could be useful in exploring possible development and articulation of regional or national outcomes.

A high-level outcome model for a Public Service Value national study could be drawn from sources such as international research studying levels of life satisfaction and happiness.[6] Other factors to include in a national outcome model might include economics, governance, society (including social factors such as marriage, divorce rates and university-level education) and the environment. In terms of cost-effectiveness, a Public Service Value national study could look at "income per head," which would represent the total monetary resources available to support all of the outcomes. Outcome scores could be normalized with respect to the all-year, all-country average scores for the relevant indicators, so that they could be meaningfully compared to each other over time.

Trends in outcomes and cost-effectiveness could be identified and analyzed, offering unique insights into whole-of-government performance. This is politically challenging, to be sure, but this type of analysis could help open up whole new discourses on effective government.

At whatever level of analysis, identifying specific changes that public service organizations can make to deliver increased public value is the key pay-off of using the Public Service Value methodology. Armed with the understanding of value drivers from a Public Service Value analysis, public managers can use this information to inform their decisions about how to allocate scarce resources to drive and improve social results.

The Key to Unlocking Public Value

We began this book by describing how public managers need new tools to respond to the "value squeeze" between rising stakeholder expectations and limited financial means. Much of the book has examined how public managers can use the Public Service Value methodology as an analytical framework to respond to these pressures and unlock public value. In this final chapter, we will explore innovation, which can be a key that public managers can use to unlock public value.

> *For the next 20 years, policy makers face hard political choices. Since most governments cannot increase their share of the economy, in some countries this will put pressure on entitlement programs. These new demands on builders of public management systems will require leadership from officials with enhanced individual, technical, managerial and political capacities who think and plan collectively and who can work well with other actors.*

This quote from a 2005 Organization for Economic Cooperation and Development report titled "Modernizing Government: The

Way Forward" highlights the need for innovation in service delivery for governments around the world to create public value.[1]

Outcomes as an Engine of Change

Innovative change in the public sector can be sparked by a re-evaluation of outcomes. By reexamining the assumptions inherent in many public services, opportunities for innovation can be uncovered.

For example, the London Police Department recently introduced an innovation in police patroling. Since 2002, police community support officers in London have been working alongside the police, patroling public spaces and providing reassurance to the public.

The need for heightened security in London after the September 11, 2001, terrorist attacks in New York City and Washington, D.C., stimulated support for ideas that had begun to develop some time before. After September 11, it became increasingly evident, most notably to Sir Ian Blair the then Deputy Commissioner of the London Metropolitan Police, that the police could not cost-effectively meet the growing demand for the patrol of public places and that this was limiting their ability to deliver the essential outcome of public reassurance of safety. In that environment, the introduction of new community support officers seemed like an idea whose time had come.

Although some initially raised concerns about community support officers not being fully trained and equipped police officers, this new type of officer has been mainly well received by the public. The Metropolitan Police Department found innovative ways to better use its resources to respond to new needs and, at the same time, public perceptions of safety improved with the increased presence of the new type of officers on the street.

The London police case is an example of an innovative reconfiguration of workforce to better achieve an outcome of the public perception of safety. Other innovations can be in the method of delivering public services. Electronic tax filing is an example of adopting online technologies to give taxpayers a new and more efficient way of filing their tax returns.

A hypothetical example of how reevaluating outcomes may spark innovation is in secondary school education. Today, most secondary schools are built around the assumption that education is delivered in schools with physical buildings that run on fixed hours with a regulated curriculum and where students are taught in age-appropriate grade levels. But, what if those assumptions of full-time schooling and the mix of school and work or other experiences are challenged and more education is delivered online? Might students learn more and be better prepared for life after school if their education were delivered differently? Are there more cost-effective ways to deliver even better secondary school education? If we take a step back and think through the fundamental outcomes we expect from education, we may come up with new ideas to test that will challenge our original assumptions and create public value.

The Public Service Value Model provides a framework that public managers can use to look for innovative ideas by challenging the assumptions that underpin each of the outcomes for a given public service.

Competitive Dynamics

In the private sector, competition can be a primary driver of change and innovation. It may be instructive to examine the dynamics of competition in the private sector to see what public service organizations can leverage.

Private sector corporations compete in two markets: the market for customers and the market for capital. To win in the market for customers, corporations try to deliver products or services that appeal to the customer and are priced attractively in comparison to other offerings from competing organizations. To win in the market for capital, corporations aim to generate an economic return on the capital employed that is equal or superior to that earned by other corporations running similar levels of risk. There are clearly both synergies and trade-offs to be had as corporations seek to be successful in both markets. A product that is attractive to customers but that cannot be produced profitably will not succeed. Equally, a product that customers do not want to purchase will not generate sales.

In a mature but competitive industry, a number of companies may compete with each other in these twin linked markets. Each seeks advantages that will either boost demand for the product or improve profitability, or both. Successful improvements are rapidly copied by competitors and so advantages gained can be eroded over time and further improvements sought.

In an efficient market (which is not always the case), competitive pressures lead to ongoing improvement in the quality of products and services delivered at acceptable levels of profitability. In a mature industry, however, the trade-offs between the twin markets for customers and capital are stronger, and improvement in performance in one might increasingly come at the expense of deteriorating performance in the other. These pressures contribute to increasingly marginal improvements in performance. At this point, "innovative" change often occurs.

Changing the Rules of the Game

Innovative change in the private sector occurs when a company challenges the fundamental assumptions that underpin the competitive status quo. The innovation may radically reshape the product in some way or produce the product with a new economic model. Successful innovation is disruptive; it changes the rules of the game. If the rules are changed, then competitors struggle to improve their performance to challenge the innovative newcomer. Either they transform their business and adopt the new market rules or they are marginalized. Such change can produce significant results such as a threefold increase in customers, a product that is a fifth of the price or profitability that is two or three times better than before.

The rise of budget airlines illustrates how innovation can change the rules in an industry. Until recently, the major airlines competed around a well-understood set of parameters as follows. Profitability largely came from business customers. Business customers, it was believed, cared about convenience and quality of service. They wanted to fly from major hub airports conveniently located in major business centers such as London, New York and Frankfurt. They wanted flexible ticketing, executive lounges, good food and so forth. For all this they were prepared to pay a relatively high price. The remainder of the plane could then be filled up with tourists at a price to clear the market but without cannibalizing the core high-paying business class traffic.

The budget airlines' innovation was to accept very different assumptions. They observed that by guaranteeing a full plane they could reduce ticket prices considerably. They recognized that by removing the "frills" deemed essential for business customers, they could cut costs, reduce ticket prices and still make a profit. They also observed that by standardizing their fleet and adopting the latest online ticketing technology, they could further reduce operating costs. But would people want to fly from secondary airports on nonflexible tickets bought online, traveling in relatively spartan conditions where "extras" are limited and perhaps even luggage was restricted? What if the ticket price was reduced not from $500 to $250, but to $100, $50 or $20? The good news for budget airlines is that the bet paid off—the new operating model did indeed allow the dramatic cuts in operating costs that would enable the low fares, which in turn would fill the planes at a profit. The budget airlines redefined both the service that airlines provided and the economic "model" used to provide those services. Such an innovative change would never have arisen from the status quo of competition among established airlines.

Creating an Appetite for Experimentation in the Public Sector

The experimentation process can be more difficult in the public sector. Returning to our budget airline example illustrates why this is so. Prior to the arrival of the budget airlines, the established airlines were competing successfully with each other around their established model. If the budget airlines had not been able to make their new model "fly," their failure would have had little or no impact on the airline industry as a whole. Their innovation was only disruptive once it was successful. Because their model did work, the rest of the industry had to respond. If the model had not worked, it would not have disrupted the airline industry long term. This example illustrates that innovation in the private sector therefore presents manageable risks for the industry as a whole. If the innovation is successful, the entire industry must adjust rapidly to accommodate the innovation. But, if an innovation is unsuccessful, the innovator will fail and soon be forgotten.

Traditionally, public service organizations have had little incentive to spend time and money on "experiments" that may fail, because that failure may affect people's lives. That said, there are examples of innovation in the public sector that we can point to and learn from, such as congestion charging, where leaders have been bold enough to experiment to improve public service delivery.

Congestion charging involves charging a toll to vehicles that enter specific areas at peak transit times with the aim of reducing overall road usage and thus relieving congestion. Although traffic congestion and growing commute times in and around London were problems for years, the cost, complexity and risk of introducing congestion charging originally deterred London public officials from taking action.

In 2000, when London elected its first mayor for the whole metropolitan area, the successful candidate, Ken Livingstone, stood on a platform of, among other things, relieving congestion and improving public transport in London. He decided in 2001 to implement a system of congestion charging to a few square miles of central London, and the system was enacted in February 2003. The solution he chose used camera recognition of license plates as well as a number of innovative payment mechanisms using the Web and short message service (SMS) text messaging from mobile phones. The introduction of the scheme in a limited area and using relatively simple technology was deliberate. The Mayor understood that for his innovation to be successful, it must take little time to implement and produce results. Once successful, the program could then be expanded.

Congestion charging in central London has already reduced commute times by more than the original target. Careful management of the introduction of the scheme minimized initial growing pains. There are now plans to extend the congestion charging zone. Other cities in the United Kingdom are also looking to replicate the innovation, and there are discussions under way about moving to more sophisticated technology.

London's congestion charging scheme illustrates how a new leader can strategically use innovation to improve public value. The mayor was prepared to try a new approach. He understood that the best way to innovative was to implement a real program and to do it on a manageable scale. He also understood that delivering demonstrable public value early, in the form of reduced congestion, would strengthen his hand in expanding the scheme later. The congestion charging scheme also illustrates that successful innovation that delivers value will generate imitation.

Creativity in Public Services

In a recent report, "Unblocking Creativity in the Public Services," the Office for Public Management (OPM), a nonprofit public service research and development organization, examines the process of innovation and creativity in the public sector. In the conclusion to the report, OPM states, "As members of the public and as service users, we all need creativity in public services. People working in creative public services are not necessarily satisfied with traditional ways of doing things. They develop approaches that enable better performance in familiar situations and they respond smartly to changes in the society they serve. Faced with new challenges, creative public services develop new ideas to apply to often complex problems, leading to improved social outcomes and the more effective use of limited resources."[2]

OPM observes that one of the forces public service organizations can tap into to drive innovation is their own workforce, which is already highly motivated to find ways to provide the public with better services. It recommends the following to encourage creativity:

- Make everyone in the organization alert to and aware of opportunities for creative change.
- Ensure that the essential ingredients for creativity are in place, including human resource policies to reward and recognize new ideas and to recruit diverse teams.
- Provide leadership to develop a climate for creativity inside an organization and its external relations.

While creativity cannot be prescribed, a comprehensive strategy, based on all of these components can provide the right conditions for creativity to flourish.

Although innovation is one of the keys to unlocking the value of public service organizations, it is often difficult to implement in the public sector due to structural constraints. One such structural constraint is the customer base. In most cases, public service organizations do not choose their customers and vice versa. For example, a tax agency has to deal with the complex tax returns as well as the routine ones. It cannot segment customers as retailers can and charge for different levels of service accordingly.

Public managers can help foster innovation by creating an environment in which experimentation in service delivery is possible; in which successful new models of service delivery can thrive and organically displace previous ones; and in which failure is neither overly disruptive to the system as a whole nor discouraging to further attempts at innovation. The risks of innovation can be reduced by implementing change in a defined environment first, as in the London congestion charge example, and also in looking for ways to restructure organizations to foster change in service delivery. For example, if monolithic organizations are divided into smaller, discrete administrative units, innovation can be tried out in a limited area before being widely propagated. Alternatively, public managers can bring the same functions from a number of organizations together into a single unit, where economies of scale and an improved management focus can help foster innovation. In addition, if legislators make funding decisions based on whether or not an organization creates increased public value, this will encourage innovative thinking and experimentation around how to increase value.

Improving public value significantly is going to require many innovations in the ways that public services are organized, managed and delivered.

Innovations must be driven by a clear understanding of the social outcomes that citizens expect from public services. In particular, this understanding must take into account the changing perceptions, visible in part through the political process, and the differing expectations that may vary significantly by communities. For example, the alleviation of disease remains one of the overall outcomes of a public health system, but what this might mean at the next level will differ between a Western country and an underdeveloped country and will change over time.

If governments can find a way to create a climate in which radical innovation in service delivery in the public sector is possible, then it is much more likely that needed innovations will occur in the public sector and that public value will be increased. This will require the creation of administrative structures that can accommodate experimentation and allow successful innovative organizations to take over, or in some other way supersede, less innovative organizations. While unsuccessful attempts at innovation must be allowed to fail, there should be no further punishment for well-intentioned, outcome-focused innovation failures; many attempts at innovation will be unsuccessful, but many of the ones that are successful are likely to make a substantial and positive difference in the lives of people they serve.

In the end, all forms of public spending need to be judged against their contribution to current and future public value. To the extent that any one item of expenditure creates greater public value than another, on the surface of it, it should be given preference. Contribution to increased public value and high performance in government should be the primary determinant of public expenditure decisions and of public management action.

Appendix

Public Service Value Methodology

The Accenture Public Service Value Model is a disciplined approach to public sector performance management focused on defining outcomes, quantifying results and identifying ways to achieve increased outcomes cost-effectively. This appendix describes a high-level work plan you can follow to put this methodology to work in your organization. We have found that what is crucially important in each step of the approach is the thinking and deliberation that application of the model prompts among public managers and their stakeholders—in many cases, even more important than the precise measures it produces. In that sense, the model really is a tool, not the answer.

The work plan of the Public Service Value Model has four stages:

1. Define Outcomes and Metrics
2. Calculate Outcome and Cost-Effectiveness Scores
3. Perform the Public Service Value Performance Matrix
4. Analyze the Public Service Value Performance Results

The Public Service Value Model evaluates Public Service Value as the total social outcome produced divided by the cost-effectiveness of the resources used (see Figure A.1).

FIGURE A.1

Public Service Value Model Calculation

Public Service Value = Outcomes ÷ Cost Effectiveness

Stage 1: Define Outcomes and Metrics

The goal of this stage is to clearly define and prioritize outcomes and develop a list of metrics that can be used to measure value created by the organization or program. At the end of this stage, you will have a Public Service Value outcome model with a short list of outcome-based performance metrics aligned to each outcome. Each outcome and metric will have a weighting assigned to it to reflect the organization's strategic priorities.

Key Activities for Stage 1

1. Research your organization's building blocks to develop a draft outcome list.
2. Hold internal workshops to validate and weight outcomes.
3. Gather and filter list of metrics with internal managers and other industry experts.

Research Your Organization's Building Blocks and Develop a Draft Outcome List

To determine what outcomes and metrics to use for your Public Service Value Model, it is helpful to use the Public Service Value building blocks (see Figure A.2). Choosing the right outcomes is crucial to the success of the analysis. The first step in developing outcomes is to define in detail the four building blocks: (1) the organization's mission or raison d'etre; (2) core functions and capabilities; (3) stakeholders/customers; and (4) stakeholders'/customers' expectations.

Sources of information for the building blocks include mission statements, governmental statutes, bylines of a nonprofit organization, citizen-based polls, surveys or focus groups and interviews with policy experts. After the building blocks have been defined, the next step is to synthesize that information into a list of outcomes that collectively answer the questions, "Why do we exist? What are the end results that this organization aims to deliver to key stakeholders?" In most cases, three to seven outcomes are sufficient to give a comprehensive and clear view of performance at the highest level. If the short list of outcomes is not comprehensive enough, it is possible to use the same process to create sub-outcomes (below a given outcome) to categorize the end results an organization strives to achieve.

FIGURE A.2

Public Service Value Building Blocks

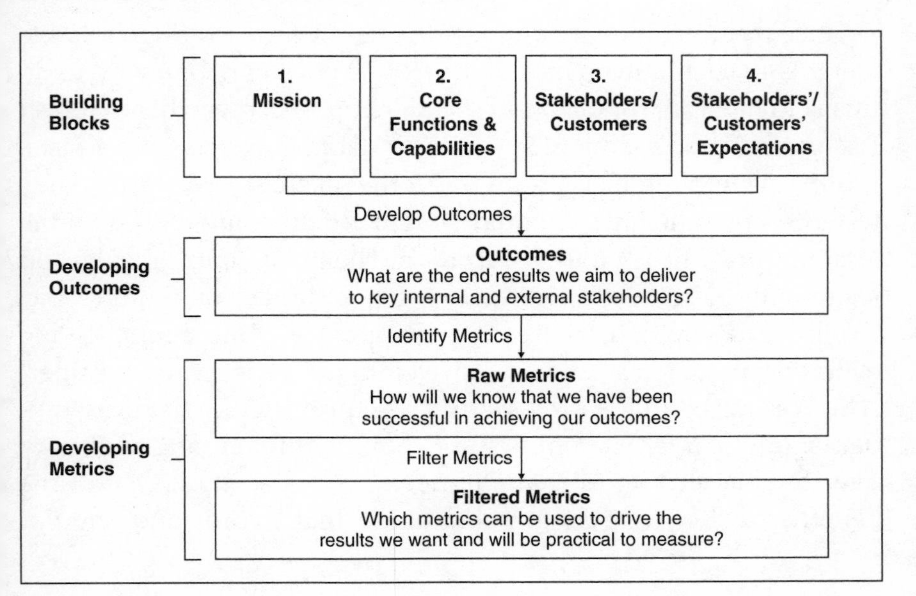

Hold Internal Workshops to Validate and Weight Outcomes

To validate that the outcomes reflect an organization's goals and are tailored to meet its needs, conduct brainstorming workshops with internal managers to review outcomes. One tool to use for the validation process is the four-part outcome filter below.

Public Service Value Outcome Filter

1. *Mission Focused*—Is the outcome aligned with the organization's mission and vision?
2. *Action Oriented*—Do the outcomes drive quantifiable improvements? Are employees held accountable for improving outcomes? Do employees understand how their actions affect outcomes?
3. *Comprehensive*—Do the outcomes, taken as a whole, reflect all of the organization's core capabilities, functions and strategies?
4. *Creates Values for Stakeholders*—Is the outcome something that the organization's stakeholders value?

Once the outcomes are defined, the next step is to assign relative weights to each outcome on a scale of 100 percent. One way to do this is to have an organization's leadership select weights to reflect the organization's strategic priorities. A voting exercise can assist a group in assigning weights. In the voting exercise, ask participants to write down how they would weight the outcomes based on the strategic priorities of the organization. Then tally up the results and share with the group, opening up a group discussion on the topic. After the discussion, ask each participant to vote again, giving everyone the chance to reassign weights to reflect any new perspectives raised in the discussion. These priorities, in turn, are fundamentally driven by politics and public opinion, and will vary over time according to changing legislative priorities. One of the benefits of this weighting technique is that it can (and should) change with the times. As priorities change, the weights can also be changed.

Gather and Filter List of Metrics with Industry Experts and Other Internal Managers

After selecting a set of outcomes, the next step in the outcome development process is to identify, filter and weight metrics that will measure whether or not an outcome is achieved. Interview industry policy experts and internal managers to come up with a list of potential metrics. Another source of potential metrics is the list of traditional performance metrics and key performance indicators that an organization is already using to track performance. But do not stop with that original list. Rather, seek metrics that pass the metrics filter below and answer the question, "Are we achieving our intended outcome?" The metrics filter is useful to identify metrics that can be used to drive desired outcomes and are also practical to measure. The metrics filter has two parts, an intentions filter and a feasibility figure, as outlined below.

Public Service Value Two-Part Metrics Filter

1. Intentions Filter
   - *Outcomes Focused*—Are the metrics measuring the "end goal" of the program or organization and not the inputs or outputs used to achieve it?
   - *Customer Focused*—Do the metrics track and measure what customers and other stakeholders value?
   - *Drives Intended Behavior*—Do the metrics drive the intended behavior?
   - *Actionable*—Does the metric give executives meaningful information to use to make decisions (to improve the outcome)?

2. Feasibility Filter
    - *Measurable*—Are the metrics quantifiable, reliable and well defined?
    - *Practical/Affordable*—Do the data currently exist? Is the cost of measurement (time and expenses) justified by the benefit of the measurement?

If metrics pass the intentions filter, but not the feasibility filter (i.e. if there are no data available for a useful metric), proxy metrics can be selected while exploring whether or not the intended metric can be implemented. Inverse ratios may also serve as effective proxies for hard-to-attain metrics. A decline in the number of complaints, for example, may serve as a proxy for an increase in customer satisfaction.

As with outcomes, each metric needs a weight assigned, and those weights can change over time to reflect changing priorities.

The final step is to take the complete model back to internal and external policy experts to validate that it will accurately measure value created and that it is tailored to meet an organization's needs (see Figure A.3). This is likely to open up considerable debate and discussion, which can be useful in thinking about future actions needed to improve performance.

Stage 2: Calculating Outcome and Cost-Effectiveness Scores

To calculate the outcome score, one important step is to review each metric to see if any data need to be adjusted so that they can be used for the outcome calculations. To adjust the data so that they can be aggregated and compared across multiple years, two techniques are used: standardization and normalization.

Standardization is a technique used to be able to compare data across multiple years. Standardization allows comparison of apples to apples to truly see the changes in data over time without being misled. For example, if you chose to standardize the metric "total number of audits for a specific year" for a revenue agency, an

FIGURE A.3

Example: Public Service Value Outcome Model

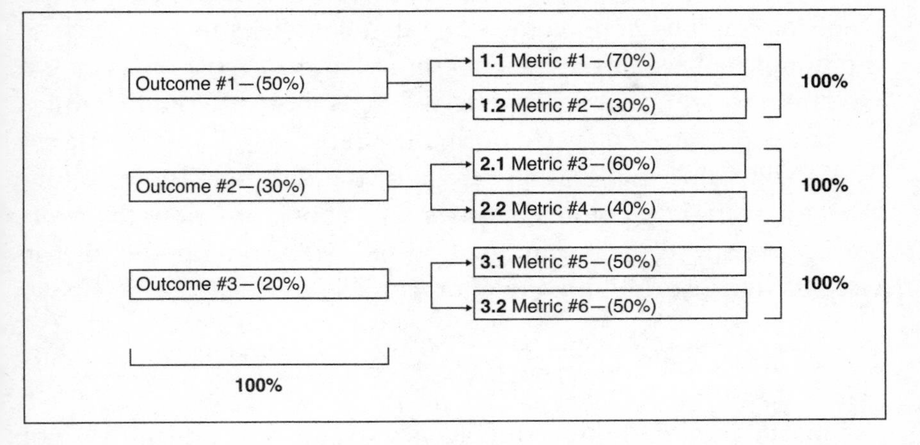

arbitrary target would be set—for example, "As a revenue agency, we must minimize the number of audits that require adjusting." The following steps would be taken to standardize the data. Though the actual number of audits each year varies, the standardized metric is the percentage of audits resulting in adjustments. These metrics can now be compared year by year. (See Table A.1.)

TABLE A.1

Example: Standardizing Data

Maximize Compliance Rates	**1997**	**1998**	**1999**	**2000**	**2001**	**2002**	**2003**
No charge audits							
Individual							
Audits requiring no adjustment	5	2	6	15	8	10	6
Total number of audits	252	231	217	216	177	207	170
Percentage of audits resulting in adjustments	**98.0%**	**99.1%**	**97.2%**	**93.1%**	**95.5%**	**95.2%**	**96.5%**

Result: All data is now comparable across years

Normalization is a technique used to be able to combine metrics of different base units. Normalization converts raw data into a form where it can be used in combination with other data. If you want to calculate an outcome score that combines metrics such as the number of welfare recipients served and the cost of serving a welfare recipient, you need to be able to combine two units: number of people and money. To normalize data, one divides a data set by a fixed value that is the average of the data set. The resulting ratio for each data point is a percentage above or below the average. Normalized data can then be added up with the metric weights to come up with a total outcome score:

Normalized score = Score / Average of all scores across data set

Table A.2 using the revenue agency example, produces a set of scores that fluctuate around the value "1," relative to the average of the data set. These scores enable you to combine measures of performance from different outcome metrics.

TABLE A.2

Example: Normalizing Data

Maximize Compliance Rates	**1997**	**1998**	**1999**	**2000**	**2001**	**2002**	**2003**
No change audits							
Individual							
Audits requiring no adjustment	5	2	6	15	8	10	6
Total number of audits	252	231	217	216	177	207	170
Percentage of audits resulting in adjustments	98.0%	99.1%	97.2%	93.1%	95.5%	95.2%	96.5%
Average = 96.37							
Normalized score	**1.02**	**1.03**	**1.01**	**0.97**	**0.99**	**0.99**	**1.00**

Calculating the Individual Outcome Score

Once outcomes and metrics have been defined and the metrics data adjusted, each individual outcome score can be calculated. This calculation involves each metric's normalized score being multiplied by its assigned weight and then aggregated to provide a total individual outcome score. For example, to generate the final outcome score from the four metrics related to "voluntary tax payers," the calculation in Table A.3 is used.

Calculating the Total Outcome Score

Once each individual outcome score has been calculated, it is then multiplied by its assigned weighting and then aggregated with other outcome scores to give a total outcome score. For example, the total 2004 outcome score for the welfare agency in Table A.4 is:

$$(1.071*35\%) + (1.056*30\%) + (1.369*20\%) + (2.11*15\%) = 1.283$$

Calculating the Cost-Effectiveness Score

The Public Service Value methodology defines cost-effectiveness as the outcomes that an organization has achieved against the cost incurred, or the ratio of outcomes generated to the amount of resources consumed/employed in producing or delivering outcomes over time. Essentially, cost-effectiveness measures the social return on public investment. Cost-effectiveness is calculated by dividing "normalized" outcomes by the adjusted cost per user (see Figure A.4).

The adjusted cost per user simply represents the total costs (operating expenditures + capital charge [adjusted for inflation]) divided by the target population. As this formula suggests, in order to accurately calculate total costs, one must take into account both the annual budget and the asset base.

The annual operating expenditure component of this is fairly intuitive. These are the day-to-day expenses incurred in running

TABLE A.3

Example: Final Metrics Score

2.1 Voluntary vs. Actual Taxpayers		1997	1998	1999	2000	2001	2002	2003
2.1.1 Individual Taxpayers (measured by tax returns)								
Individual taxpayers (measured by tax returns in 000)		2,836	2,872	2,918	3,117	3,051	3,028	3,056
Taxpayers per employed member of labor force		0.94	0.95	0.97	1.02	1.01	0.99	0.99
Normalized Public Service Value score		**0.956**	**0.970**	**0.987**	**1.040**	**1.029**	**1.009**	**1.009**
2.1.2 Corporate Taxpayers (measured by tax returns)								
Corporate taxpayers (measured by tax returns in 000)		n/a	157	176	179	184	175	175
Corporate taxpayers per business		0.37	0.37	0.41	0.41	0.42	0.40	0.40
Normalized Public Service Value score		**0.931**	**0.931**	**1.032**	**1.036**	**1.057**	**1.005**	**1.005**
2.1.3 Sales & Use Compliant Taxpayers								
Sales & use compliant taxpayers (in 000)		n/a	n/a	118	109	112	117	n/a
Compliant taxpayer per total taxpayer count		0.65	0.65	0.65	0.60	0.62	0.64	0.64
Normalized Public Service Value score		**1.023**	**1.023**	**1.023**	**0.942**	**0.973**	**1.008**	**1.008**
2.1.4 Withholding Compliant Taxpayers								
Withholding compliant taxpayers (in 000)		n/a	n/a	119	109	115	121	n/a
Compliant taxpayer per total taxpayer count		0.71	0.71	0.71	0.64	0.66	0.69	0.69
Normalized Public Service Value score		**1.033**	**1.033**	**1.033**	**0.929**	**0.964**	**1.003**	**1.003**
2.1 Weighted Score Voluntary vs. Actual Taxpayers								
2.1.1 Individual taxpayers (measured by tax returns)	**24.7%**	0.96	0.97	0.99	1.04	1.03	1.01	1.01
2.1.2 Corporate taxpayers (measured by tax returns)	**10.0%**	0.93	0.93	1.03	1.04	1.06	1.01	1.01
2.1.3 Sales & use compliant taxpayers	**40.7%**	1.02	1.02	1.02	0.94	0.97	1.01	1.01
2.1.4 Withholding compliant taxpayers	**24.7%**	1.03	1.03	1.03	0.93	0.96	1.00	1.00
Weighted average score	**100%**	**1.000**	**1.004**	**1.018**	**0.972**	**0.993**	**1.007**	**1.007**

Final metric score for the year 2000: (1.04 * 25%) + (1.04 * 10%) + (0.94 * 41%) + (0.93 * 25%) = 0.972

the organization, such as utilities, office supplies, salaries, bonuses, contract labor, insurance, postage, repairs, administration, marketing, research and development, travel, training, depreciation and amortization, short-term projects and other expenses not exceeding one year.

The concept of a capital charge on the asset base comes from the

TABLE A.4

Example: Total Outcome Score Calculation

	2001	2002	2003	2004	Weighting
1. Maximize health through the utilization of preventive services	0.967	0.976	0.983	1.071	35%
2. Maximize access	0.918	0.973	1.053	1.056	30%
3. Optimize revenue and medical costs	0.602	0.841	1.168	1.369	20%
4. Minimize administrative burden	0.587	0.599	0.699	2.11	15%
Total outcome score	**0.822**	**0.892**	**1.003**	**1.283**	**n/a**
Percentage deviation from the mean	-17.8%	-10.8%	3%	28.3%	n/a

Overall Outcome Scores

Outcome Weightings

notion of opportunity cost. If a public service organization is holding assets, it is holding onto resources that could hypothetically be used for other public services. The return that a public service organization could get from these assets, if the organization did not

FIGURE A.4

Cost-Effectiveness Calculation

Cost-Effectiveness is a return on investment calculation that is a ratio of outcomes generated to the amount of resources consumed in producing these outcomes. It measures how effectively an agency utilizes its resources. The Capital Charge represents the opportunity cost of holding capital that could be invested elsewhere.

Cost-Effectiveness = Outcome Score ÷ (Operating Expenses + Capital Charge)

hold them, can be approximated to the government bond rate. Current liabilities are subtracted from the equation because total assets minus current liabilities are the true level of assets or capital employed by the organization. Current liabilities are the debt that is being used to operate the business on a daily basis, but not the funds that are used to help the organization to achieve its outcomes.

Financial Adjustments Required to Calculate Cost-Effectiveness

1. *Calculating the Capital Charge.* Within a country, for example, the United Kingdom, the cost of debt in the public sector is consistent across government bodies because it is borne centrally by Her Majesty's Treasury. Given this cost of debt, the prevailing 10-year government bond rate can be used to calculate the capital charge. Multiplying the total assets of the organization, less current liabilities, by this rate will provide an estimate of the capital charge or the government's cost of holding assets (see Figure A.5).
2. *Determining Inflation Rates.* In our cost-effectiveness calculations, total costs are discounted by the compounded rate of inflation. Depending on the country and the organization's sensitivity around the topic, the level of complexity required in calculating inflation can vary considerably. For instance, for a health organization, determining the inflation index may require a study of changes in prices for prescription

FIGURE A.5

Capital Charge Calculation

Capital Charge = (Total Assets - Current Liabilities) x Cost of Capital

drugs, health insurance, primary care services, surgical treatments, long-term care assistance, changes in human capital supplies (i.e. nurses and doctors) and so forth. The compounded inflation rate of all of these variables will produce a real rate of inflation for that specific industry (see Table A.5). The cumulative rate of inflation represents the current year's inflation rate multiplied by the previous year's inflation. The adjusted cost expenditure is the current total cost expenditure divided by the cumulative rate of inflation.

3. *Converting Cash Accounting to Accrual Accounting.* The accounting principles used by an organization affect the way expenses are reported in their financial statements. Organizations using accrual-based accounting, or the matching concept, assume that income is recognized or accrued as it is earned (regardless of when the money is received) and expenses are reported when they are incurred (regardless of whether they are paid or not). If an organization follows an accrual-based accounting system, there is no need for adjustments because income and expenses relate to the same years in which the outcomes were achieved. However, if an organization uses a cash-based accounting system, it records income when cash is received and expenses when they are paid. As a result, it fails to recognize the true value of the assets purchased because it records all expenses/ investments as an expense against the annual budget in the year

TABLE A.5

Example: Inflation rate Adjustment

Adjusting for Inflation	Calculation	Year 1 (a)	Year 2 (b)	Year 3 (c)	Year 4 (d)
Total cost expenditure	Operating expenditure + capital charge	118.3	133.5	139.3	144.9
Rate of inflation	Data from National Statistical Agency	3.2%	3.0%	1.5%	2.4%
Cumulative rate of inflation	a3=1, b3=a3*(1+b2), c3=b3*(1+c2), etc.	1	1.030	1.045	1.071
Adjusted cost expenditure	**a4=a1/a3, b4=b1/b3, c4=b1/b3, etc.**	**118.3**	**129.6**	**133.2**	**135.4**

that the expense is incurred (thereby failing to recognize a useful life greater than one year). If an organization uses cash accounting, it is necessary to make several accounting reconciliations to match the money spent on these assets with the years that benefit from the expense—one must adjust cash accounting figures to reflect accrual accounting's matching principle. At a high level, the way to convert from cash to accrual accounting is to separate all long-term asset expenditures from the operating costs and capitalize them on the balance sheet, develop a depreciation schedule, add back depreciation, calculate the asset value and finally use this figure to determine the capital charge. A summary of the adjustments required according to accounting method is given in Table A.6.

4. *Accounting for Off Balance Sheet Activity.* Public service organizations are increasingly recording off balance sheet activity. Given the nature of the information contained within the financial statements of government bodies, one must consider whether adjustments should be made to these figures in

TABLE A.6

Accounting Adjustment Summary

Public Service Value-Accounting Adjustments	Accruals Accounting	Cash Accounting
Annual expenditure	No action / adjustments required	The depreciation charge must be added to the annual expenditure
Balance sheet	Check for off balance sheet activity	Build a balance sheet capitalize assets
Capital expenditure	No action / adjustments required	The capital expenditure should be subtracted from annual expenditure
Capital charge	Multiply (Total assets – Current liabilities) by the cost of capital	Capitalize the capital expenditure, depreciate accordingly, and multiply the capital employed by the cost of capital

order to provide a realistic assessment of cost-effectiveness. Specific areas where adjustments might be required to determine the most "fair" level of resources consumed by a government body include operating leases, unfunded pensions and private finance initiatives. For example, when an operating lease is material to the organization's overall expenditure and the cost of the lease plus the length of lease is known, the lease should be capitalized onto the balance sheet. For this, net present value is calculated by discounting future cash flows according to the organization's cost of capital. Then, the asset is depreciated over the life of the operating lease and that expense added back to the income statement. Finally, the capital charge on the operating lease is calculated by subtracting the value of the asset of net present value of future cash flows to the prior year accumulated depreciation. An example is given in Table A.7 of how to bring an operating lease back onto the balance sheet.

5. *Adjusting for Variances to the Population Level (or Customer Base).* The required level of expenditures is typically a prod-

TABLE A.7

Example: Accounting for Off Balance Sheet Activity

	Year 0	Year 1	Year 2	Year 3
Rental lease	10,000	5,000	5,000	5,000
Cost of capital	10.0%	10.0%	10.0%	10.0%
Discount factor	1.00	1.10	1.21	1.33
Net present value (NPV) of each payment	10,000	4,545	4,132	3,757
Total NPV	**22,434**			

	Year 0	Year 1	Year 2	Year 3
Depreciation charged	**5,609**	**5,609**	**5,609**	**5,609**
Accumulated depreciation	5,609	11,217	16,826	22,434
Net value asset beginning of year	**22,434**	**16,826**	**11,217**	**5,609**
Cost of capital	10.00%	10.00%	10.00%	10.00%
Capital charge on lease	**2,243**	**1,683**	**1,122**	**561**

uct of the population served (e.g. U.S. Internal Revenue Service requires a larger budget than the Canadian Revenue Service because the United States has a much larger base of taxpayers). Therefore, when calculating cost-effectiveness, one must consider the target audience/population served by the government organization. For example, for a police force, this might be all the citizens within a particular region, whereas the target audience for a revenue agency in the same region would only be the citizens and businesses who pay taxes (taxpayers). An example is given in Table A.8 of adjusting total costs for variances to the population level or customer base.

Putting It All Together: Calculating Total Cost-Effectiveness

Table A.9 is an example of how the cost-effectiveness score would be calculated for an organization using a cash accounting principle.

Stage 3: Creating the Public Service Value Performance Matrix and Analyzing Results

Once the outcome scores and cost-effectiveness score have been calculated, the results can be plotted on the Public Service Value

TABLE A.8

Example: Adjusting Total Costs (Operating + Capital Charge) by Number of Taxpayers

	1997	1998	1999	2000	2001	2002	2003
Total Adjusted Costs (in USD 000)	42,195	50,826	47,859	50,500	51,329	47,458	47,853
Total Number of Taxpayers (in 000)	3,231	3,266	3,331	3,513	3,461	3,442	3,470
Adjusted Cost per Person	**$13.06**	**$15.56**	**$14.37**	**$14.37**	**$14.83**	**$13.79**	**$13.79**

TABLE A.9

Example: Calculating Total Cost-Effectiveness Using Cash Accounting

	1997	1998	1999	2000	2001	2002	2003
Operating Costs (000s)							
+ Total administrative expenditure	45,274	57,042	54,518	52,636	54,452	48,213	51,259
– Capital expenditures	-5,403	-8,780	-9,561	-3,258	-3,176	-214	-1,494
– Leasing expenditures	-424	-443	-560	-2,029	-2,013	-1,797	-1,532
+ Depreciation expense - capital expenditure	1,843	2,620	3,746	4,131	4,276	3,978	3,971
= Operating expenses (a)	**41,290**	**50,438**	**48,142**	**51,682**	**53,539**	**50,180**	**52,203**
Capital Charge							
+ Capital charge for capital investment	502	798	1,048	1,262	1,043	885	612
+ Capital charge on lease (implied asset)	404	434	502	1,295	2,021	1,905	1,665
= Total capital charge (b)	**905**	**1,231**	**1,550**	**2,557**	**3,064**	**2,790**	**2,277**
Adjusted for Inflation							
Total adjusted expenditure (a+b)	**42,195**	**51,669**	**49,692**	**54,239**	**56,603**	**52,970**	**54,480**
Underlying inflation rate	2.4%	1.7%	2.1%	3.4%	2.7%	1.2%	2.0
Price index	1	1.02	1.04	1.07	1.10	1.12	1.14
Expenditure adjustment for inflation and capital charge	**42,195**	**50,826**	**47,859**	**50,500**	**51,329**	**47,458**	**47,853**
Adjusted Cost per Taxpayer							
Total number of taxpayers	3,231	3,266	3,331	3,513	3,461	3,442	3,470
Adjusted cost per person	**$13.06**	**$15.56**	**$14.37**	**$14.37**	**$14.83**	**$13.79**	**$13.79**
Normalized cost score	**0.916**	**1.092**	**1.008**	**1.008**	**1.040**	**0.967**	**0.968**

performance matrix. The Public Service Value performance matrix does not present an absolute, or even a specific, measure. It provides a relative indicator of performance of an organization over time and, when appropriate, between organizations. Most important, it illustrates how an organization performs in the years covered by the analysis in terms of delivering both outcomes and cost-effectiveness. It also includes the concept of the average performance year. That is, each year is plotted on both axes as the deviation from the average performance score of outcomes and cost-effectiveness for the period of the analysis. The average performance is a score of "1" for both outcomes and cost-effectiveness. The Public Service Value performance matrix plots relative scores rather than absolutes. As such, the scores may be used to identify trends and changes in performance, and to compare against average performance over time. Note that the Public Service Value performance matrix does not set out a mathematical relationship between x (cost-effectiveness deviation) and y (outcome deviation). It merely plots the two measures of performance alongside each other (see Figure A.6).

Without changing the relative positions of the scores, the center point of the graph is made to be (0, 0), by subtracting 1 from all values (see Figure A.7). This then illustrates the percentage deviation of each score from the average score.

The Public Service Value performance matrix creates a baseline for comparing the performance of a public sector organization by examining relative change over time. It does not indicate whether an organization is performing well or badly in absolute terms, but rather whether an organization is performing better or worse than it did the year before.

A public manager would be able to look at the performance trajectory for the organization represented by the matrix below (see Figure A.8) and identify the strategic decisions that led to a significant increase in the outcomes and cost-effectiveness scores from 2001 through 2003. Likewise, the decline in both cost-effectiveness and outcomes between 1997 and 1998 might highlight the negative, albeit temporary, impact of steps taken to prepare for the subsequent performance recovery, such as making up-front investments in staff, facilities or programs that take time to bear fruit.

By definition, the Public Service Value Model measures results by comparing them to an average for all performance years being studied. Therefore, some results will be above average, and some below. The four quadrants depicted in Figure A.9 characterize in general terms the performance of organizations in terms of their ability to achieve outcomes and cost-effectiveness. Organizations landing in the upper right-hand quadrant for a particular year relative to the average are creating value in terms of increasing both outcomes and cost-effectiveness. In the upper left-hand quadrant, outcomes are increasing while cost-effectiveness is eroding. Every

FIGURE A.6

Example: Public Service Value Performance Matrix

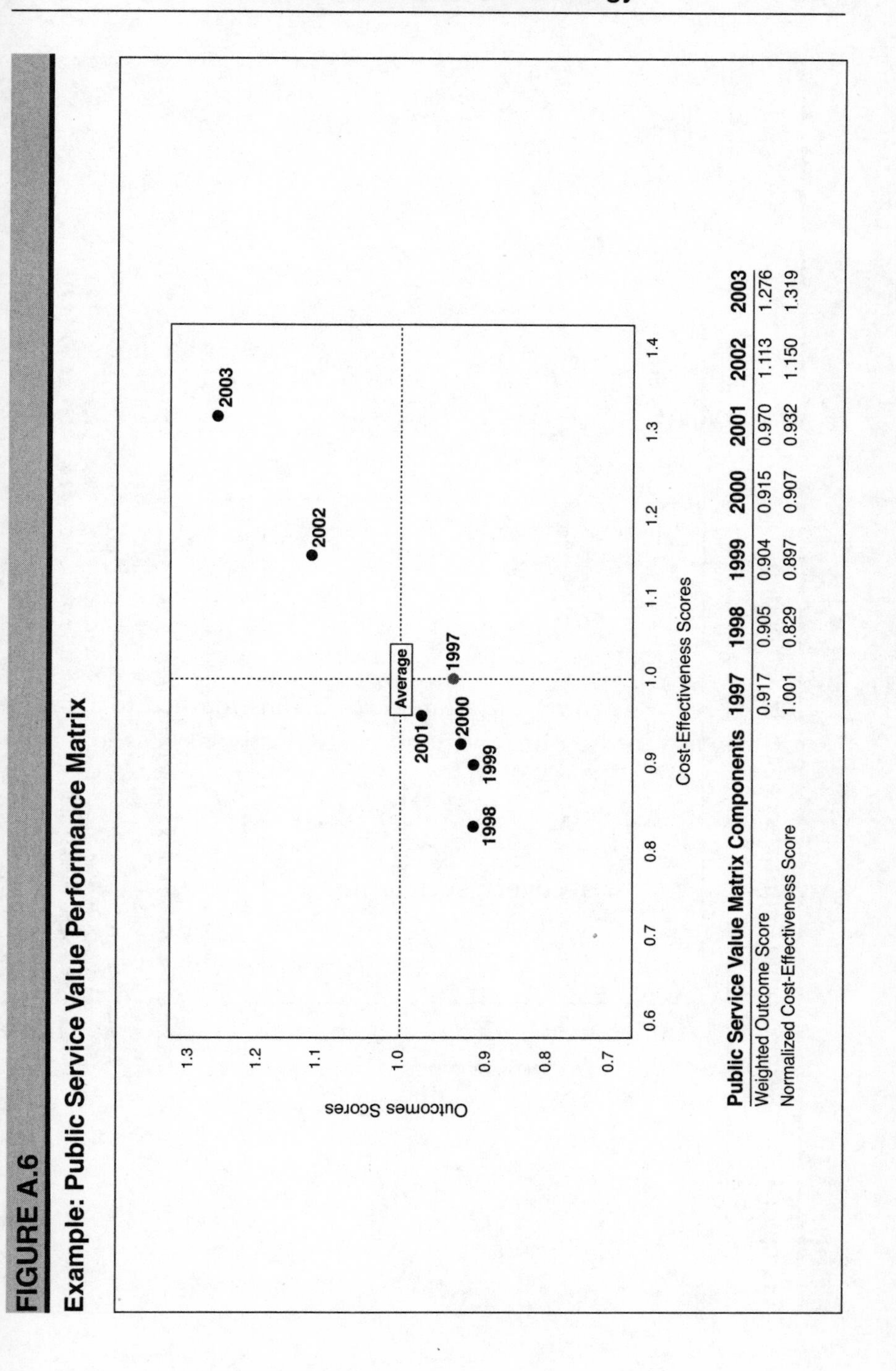

Public Service Value Matrix Components	1997	1998	1999	2000	2001	2002	2003
Weighted Outcome Score	0.917	0.905	0.904	0.915	0.970	1.113	1.276
Normalized Cost-Effectiveness Score	1.001	0.829	0.897	0.907	0.932	1.150	1.319

FIGURE A.7

Example: Public Service Value Performance Matrix (0,0 origin)

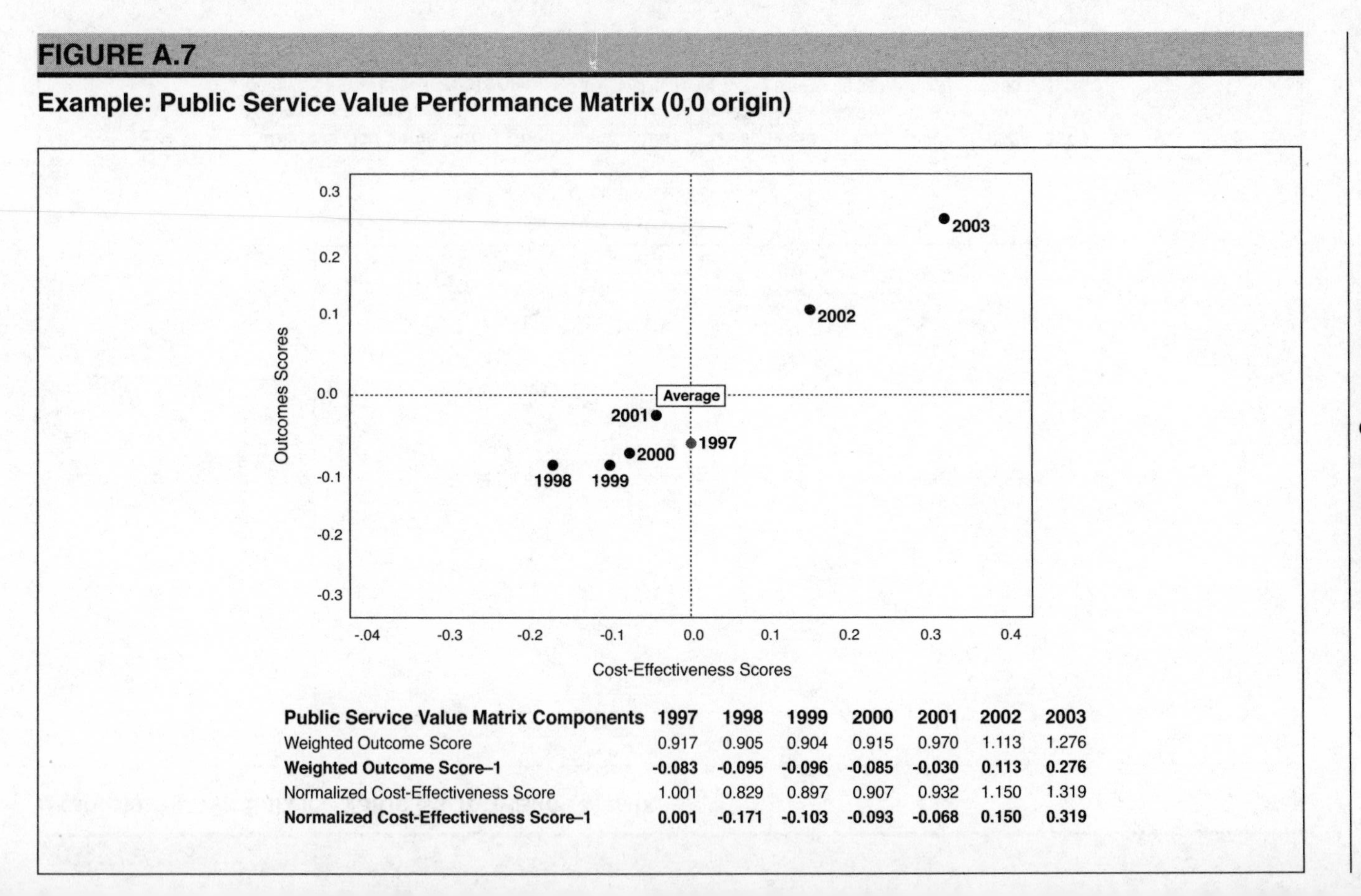

Public Service Value Matrix Components	**1997**	**1998**	**1999**	**2000**	**2001**	**2002**	**2003**
Weighted Outcome Score	0.917	0.905	0.904	0.915	0.970	1.113	1.276
Weighted Outcome Score–1	**-0.083**	**-0.095**	**-0.096**	**-0.085**	**-0.030**	**0.113**	**0.276**
Normalized Cost-Effectiveness Score	1.001	0.829	0.897	0.907	0.932	1.150	1.319
Normalized Cost-Effectiveness Score–1	**0.001**	**-0.171**	**-0.103**	**-0.093**	**-0.068**	**0.150**	**0.319**

FIGURE A.8

Public Service Value Performance Matrix (% deviation from average Public Service Value Score (FY 1997–FY2003)

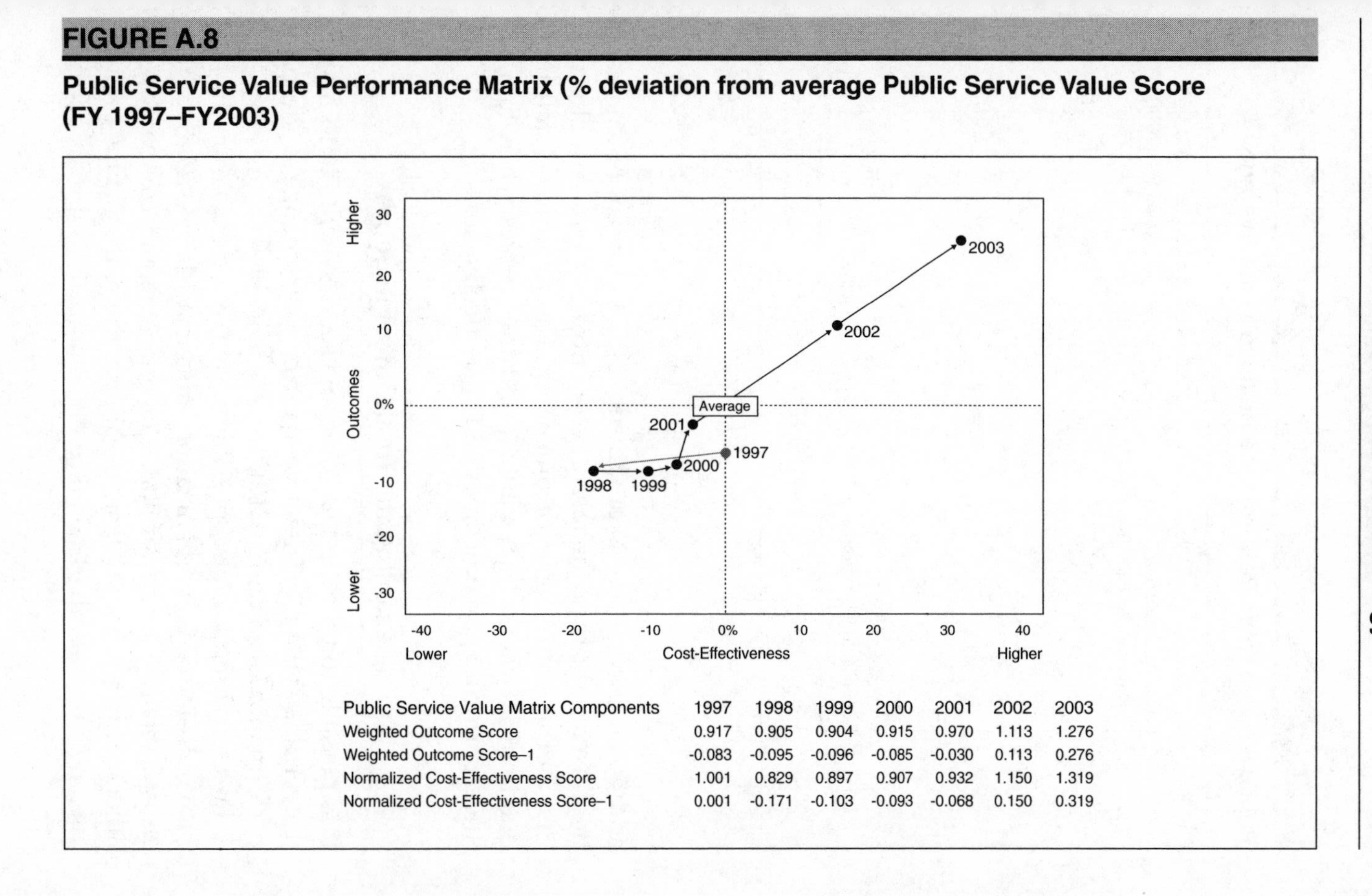

Public Service Value Matrix Components	1997	1998	1999	2000	2001	2002	2003
Weighted Outcome Score	0.917	0.905	0.904	0.915	0.970	1.113	1.276
Weighted Outcome Score–1	-0.083	-0.095	-0.096	-0.085	-0.030	0.113	0.276
Normalized Cost-Effectiveness Score	1.001	0.829	0.897	0.907	0.932	1.150	1.319
Normalized Cost-Effectiveness Score–1	0.001	-0.171	-0.103	-0.093	-0.068	0.150	0.319

FIGURE A.9

Public Service Value Performance Relative to the Average

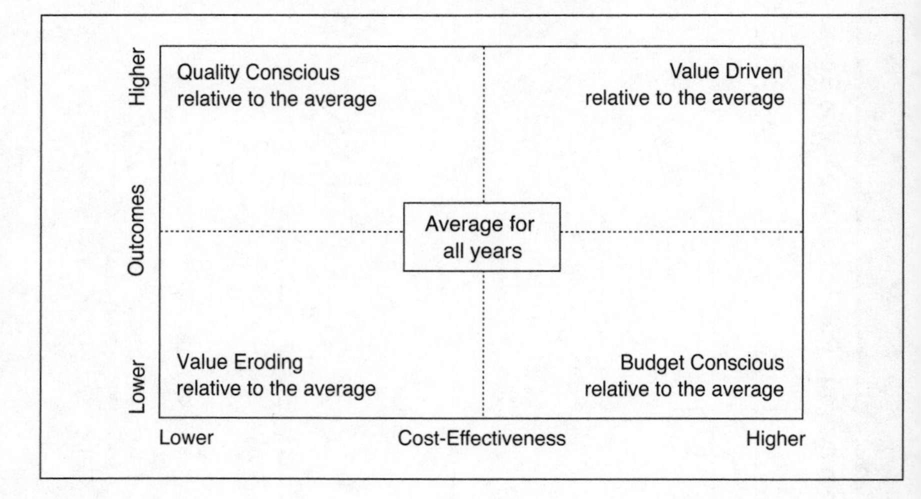

additional expenditure is producing less in terms of outcomes. In the lower right-hand quadrant, cost-cutting boosts cost-effectiveness but at the expense of outcomes. The final, lower left-hand quadrant is where organizations find themselves when they are underperforming in outcomes and cost-effectiveness.

Dissecting the Total Outcome Score

It is possible to plot the total outcome score separately to make a deeper analysis of the relative, year-on-year change in outcome performance (see Figure A.10).

Furthermore, it is also possible to make a detailed analysis of each outcome so that organizations may consider the relative, year-on-year change in performance of one outcome compared with others. This type of analysis highlights the relationships between outcomes or initiatives taken in an attempt to improve perform-

FIGURE A.10

Example: Total Outcome Score Bar Chart

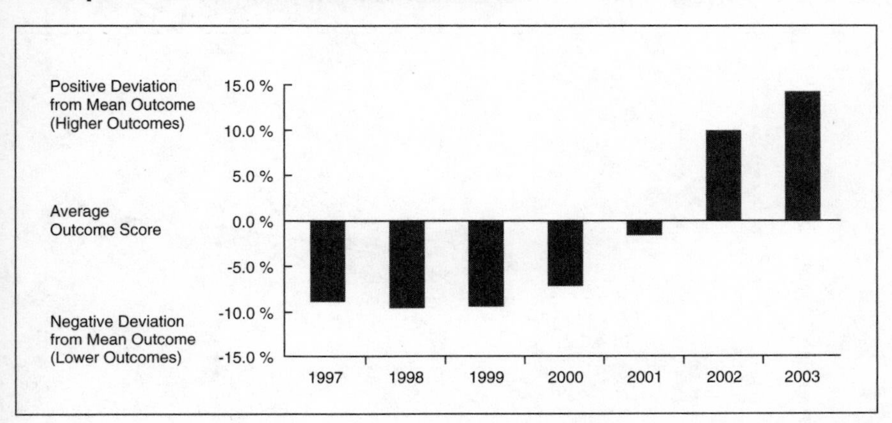

ance. Public managers also are able to examine specific areas of over- or underperformance. In Figure A.11, even though the total outcome score is improving between 1996 and 2002, outcome 2 is deteriorating in performance.

Dissecting the Cost-Effectiveness Score

It is also possible to plot the total cost-effectiveness score separately to enable a deeper analysis of the relative, year-on-year change in performance (see Figure A.12).

Using Public Service Value for Future Planning

The Public Service Value Model can be used as a framework to map out the potential impact of resource allocation decisions on future results. As such, it can serve as a valuable tool in strategic planning. In deciding between several different paths forward, the Public Service Value Model can be a useful reference point to question what impact, if any, a given decision will have on future achievement of each outcome and overall cost-effectiveness. It can also be

FIGURE A.11

Example: Analyzing Individual Outcome Performance

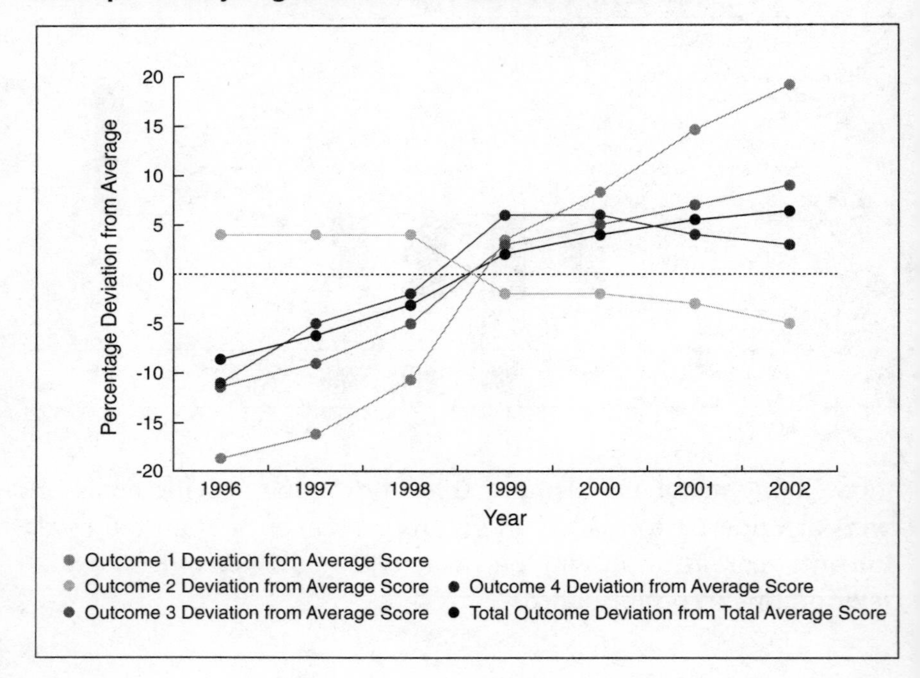

used to explore the implications of shifts in policy direction or changes in the social or economic environment. In this way, the Public Service Value Model is a tool public managers can use to play out future scenarios and evaluate their potential impact on achieving outcomes such as minimizing the burden to taxpayers in a revenue agency and doing so efficiently.

The accumulated performance results of a Public Service Value analysis can also be reviewed to uncover the value levers that were used by an organization to achieve outcomes more efficiently.

FIGURE A.12

Example: Cost-Effectiveness Bar Chart

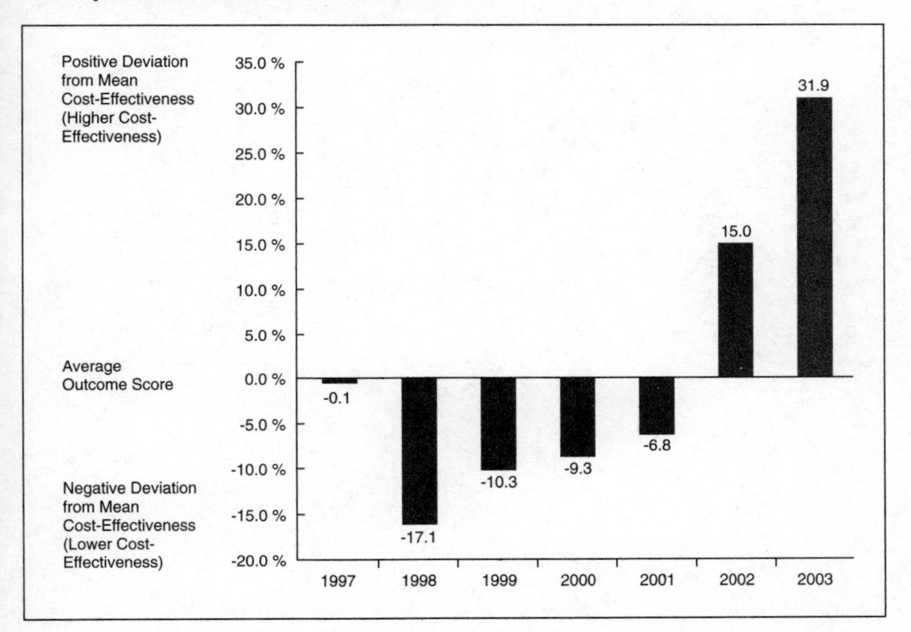

Notes

Preface

1. The Accenture Public Service Value Model is patent pending in the U.S. and Europe.

Chapter 1

1. Congressional Budget Office, *The Long-Term Budget Outlook*, December 2005, 10; and 2005 interview with Brian Riedl, analyst with Heritage Foundation.
2. David Osborne and Peter Hutchinson, *The Price of Government* (New York: Basic Books, 2004), 43.
3. Ibid., 44.
4. Ibid., 46–48.
5. For the purposes of this example we have had to simplify a very complex subject. More information on the subject can be found in the source documents at www.defra.gov.uk.
6. www.defra.gov.uk/footandmouth/cases/statistics.
7. See the U.K. Government Department of Food Agriculture and Rural Affairs (DEFRA) web site, at www.defra.gov.uk/footandmouth, for more detailed statistics and inquiries into the cause of the outbreak, the effectiveness of measures taken and lessons to be learned.
8. *Leadership in Customer Service: New Expectations, New Experiences* (Accenture, Copyright 2005), 5.
9. Ibid., 60–61.
10. Stephen Goldsmith and William D. Eggers, *Governing by Network: The New Shape of the Public Sector* (Washington: Brookings Institution Press, 2004), 13.
11. The information concerning privatization in New Zealand is based primarily on interviews conducted with Maurice McTigue, the New Zealand cabinet minister officer who led much of the privatization, by the Accenture Public Service Value team in 2005. A December 2004 review of privatization in New Zealand by the New Zealand Business Roundtable may be found at http://www.nzbr.org.nz/documents/policy/policy-2004/PB_No5.pdf.

Chapter 2

1. Theodore Poister, *Measuring Performance in Public and Nonprofit Organizations* (San Francisco: Jossey-Bass, 2003), 38.
2. General information about public service agreements and agreements for specific years may be found online at http://www.cabinetoffice.gov.uk/about_the_cabinet_office/publicserviceagreements.asp.
3. Canada's goals for its Management Account Framework are discussed on the web site of the Treasury Board of Canada Secretariat at http://www.tbs-sct.gc.ca/maf-crg/documents/bookletlivret/booklet-livret_e.asp.
4. Ibid.
5. Details of the various ways in which Singapore measures government performance are available at http://www.spring.gov.sg/portal/products/awards/sqa/sqa_indicators.html.
6. Information concerning Japan's government performance management objectives may be found at http://www.soumu.go.jp/english/kansatu/evaluation/index.html.
7. Information on France's La Loi Organique Relative aux Lois de Finances, LOLF, may be found at http://www.education.gouv.fr/dossier/lolf/.
8. Philip von Haehling, "Public Sector Strategic Performance Management: Irresolvable Dilemma or Manageable Change?" *MBA Management Project Report*, NIMBAS Graduate School of Management, Bradford University School of Management (Utrecht: NIMBAS, 2005), 37–38. German government performance measurement information also may be found at http://www.oecd.org/dataoecd/10/0/1902398.pdf. In addition, see Organization for Economic Cooperation and Development, "Models of Public Budgeting and Accounting Reform," *OECD Journal on Budgeting* 2(Suppl. 1).
9. For an overview of GPRA, see: http://www.doi.gov/gpra/.
10. Details of the President's Management Agenda may be found at http://www.whitehouse.gov/omb/budintegration/pma_index.html; for details of PART, see http://www.whitehouse.gov/omb/part/index.html.
11. *Results-Oriented Government. GPRA Has Established a Solid Foundation for Achieving Greater Results* (US GAO, 2004). To access the GAO study, see http://www.gao.gov/new.items/d0438.pdf.
12. Ibid., 8.

13. Robert S. Kaplan and David P. Norton, *The Strategy-Focused Organization—How Balanced Scorecard Companies Thrive in the New Business Environment* (Boston: Harvard Business School Press, 2000).
14. Mark H. Moore, *The Public Value Scorecard: A Rejoinder and an Alternative to "Strategic Performance Measurement and Management in Non-Profit Organizations" by Robert Kaplan,* Hauser Center for Nonprofit Organizations Working Paper No. 18, May 2003, 5. This paper may be downloaded without charge from the Social Science Research Network Electronic Paper Collection at http://ssrn.com/abstract+402880.
15. Ibid., 8–9.
16. Robert Kaplan and David Norton, "Having Trouble with Your Strategy? Then Map It," *Harvard Business Review*, September–October 2000.

Chapter 3

1. A report on the status of the Toledo Agreement may be found at http://europa.eu.int/comm/employment_social/missoc/2004/012004/es_en.pdf
2. Information concerning Spain's Instituto Nacional de la Seguridad Social, INSS, was drawn in part from interviews with Accenture executives Manuel Torres and José Rojas Seguido.
3. Robert D. Behn, "Why Measure Performance? Different Purposes Require Different Measures," *Public Administration Review*, 63, no. 5 (September–October 2003), 587.
4. Stephen Goldsmith and William Eggers, *Governing by Network: The New Shape of the Public Sector* (Washington, D.C.: The Brookings Institution, 2004), 21.
5. Changes in policing undertaken by the Greater Manchester Police discussed here and in the following paragraphs are described in detail in several reports available on the GMP web site at http://www.gmpa.gov.uk/site/publications/policingplan.htm.

Chapter 4

1. A good jumping off point for a discussion of British government initiatives relating to enhancing public sector productivity may be found at http://www.hm-treasury.gov.uk/documents/enterprise

_and_productivity/public_services_productivity/ent_services_index.cfm.

2. Information on civic initiatives in Coral Springs, Florida, may be accessed at http://www.coralsprings.org/.

Chapter 5

1. For more information on Ontario's health care initiatives, see http://www.health.gov.on.ca/.
2. Details of Washington state's performance measurement initiative, the Treatment and Report Generation Tool, or TARGET, may be found at http://www1.dshs.wa.gov/dasa/services/target/T2KMain.shtml.
3. It is worth noting that while we are stripping out the effects of inflation in this instance, we are defining a relationship to the cost of capital in the above paragraph that is a *nominal* rate, that is, one set by market factors that reflect inflationary expectations.
4. One way to approach this issue is to perform a "strategic investment" adjustment for significant, long-term investments. In this adjustment, the entity would "meter" in capital at a rate commensurate with the expectations for additional positive outcomes. For instance, if a particular $10 million investment was expected to result in 25 percent of its benefits realized in year 1, another 25 percent in year 2, and the remaining 50 percent in year 3, we would charge for only $2.5 million in year 1, $5 million in year 2, and the entire amount beginning in year 3.

Chapter 6

1. David Osborne and Peter Hutchinson, *The Price of Government* (New York: Basic Books, 2004), 169.
2. For more information on Baltimore's CitiStat initiative, see http://www.baltimorecity.gov/news/citistat/reports.html.
3. www.accenture.com/publicservicevalue.
4. *Modernizing Government: The Way Forward* (OECD, 2005), available at http://www.oecd.org/home/0,2987,en_2649_201185_1_1_1_1_1,00.html.
5. Ibid., 200.
6. Many international studies have been conducted on levels of life satisfaction/happiness within and between countries, and differences

between them have been correlated with a series of explanatory variables. Results are remarkably similar between studies and from one country and culture to the next. Most studies suggest that the variables with the greatest correlation with differences in happiness scores are: quality and stability of relationships, especially family/long-term relationships; health; security, physical and economic; and governance, including freedom, democracy, and the rule of law.

Chapter 7

1. OECD report, 205–206.
2. Jane Steel and Kerri Hampton, *Unblocking Creativity in Public Services* (OPM, 2005) 39.

Bibliography

Governance, Accountability, Innovation and Community

Albert, Michel. 1992. *Capitalism against Capitalism.* London: Whurr.

Been, Robert D. 2001. *Rethinking Democratic Accountability.* Washington, D.C.: The Brookings Institution.

Beveridge, Sir William. 1942. *Social Insurance and Allied Services (The Beveridge Report).* London: HMSO.

Collins, James C. 2001. *Good to Great—Why Some Companies Make the Leap and Others Don't.* New York: HarperCollins.

Dore, Ronald Philip. 2000. *Stock Market Capitalism: Welfare Capitalism—Japan and Germany versus the Anglo-Saxons.* Oxford, U.K.: Oxford University Press.

Goldsmith, Stephen, and William Eggers. 2004. *Governing by Network—The New Shape of the Public Sector.* Washington, D.C.: The Brookings Institution.

Layard, Richard. 2005. *Happiness—Lessons from a New Science.* New York: The Penguin Press.

Putnam, Robert D. 2000. *Bowling Alone: The Collapse and Revival of American Community.* New York: Simon & Schuster.

Tidd, Joe, John Bessant, and Keith Pavitt. 2001 *Managing Innovation—Integrating Technological, Market and Organizational Change,* 2nd ed. New York: John Wiley & Sons.

Public Management Reform—Overviews

Drucker, Peter F. 1990. *Managing the Non-Profit Organization—Principles and Practices.* New York: HarperCollins.

Moore, Mark H. 1995. *Creating Public Value—Strategic Management in Government.* Cambridge, MA: Harvard University Press.

Organization for Economic Cooperation and Development. 2005. *Modernising Government—The Way Forward.* Paris: OECD.

Osborne, David, and Peter Plastrik. 1997. *Banishing Bureaucracy—The Five Strategies for Reinventing Government.* Reading, MA: Plume.

Osborne, David, and Ted Gaebler. 1993. *Reinventing Government—How the Entrepreneurial Spirit Is Transforming the Public Sector.* Reading, MA: Plume.

Public Management Reform—Specific Topics

Bovaird, Tony, and Elke Löffler. 2003. *Public Management and Governance.* London: Routledge.

Holzer, Marc, and Seok-Hwan Lee. 2004. *Public Productivity Handbook*, 2nd ed. New York: Marcel Dekker.

Johnson, Gerry, and Kevan Scholes. 2001. *Exploring Public Sector Strategy.* Harlow, Essex, U.K.: Financial Times/Prentice Hall.

Kamensky, John M., and Albert Morales. 2005. *Managing for Results 2005.* Lanham, Maryland: Rowman & Littlefield.

Kelly, Gavin, Geoff Mulgan, and Stephen Muers. 2002. *Creating Public Value—An Analytical Framework for Public Service Reform.* London: U.K. Cabinet Office Strategy Unit.

Kettl, Donald F., and John J. Dilulio. 1995. *Inside the Reinvention Machine—Appraising Governmental Reform.* Washington, D.C.: The Brookings Institution.

Klitgaard, Robert, and Paul C. Light. 2005. *High Performance Government—Structure Leadership, Incentives.* Santa Monica, California: RAND.

Liou, Kuotsai Tom. 2001. *Handbook of Public Management Practice and Reform.* New York: Marcel Dekker.

Organization for Economic Cooperation and Development. 2002. Models of public budgeting and accounting reform. *OECD Journal on Budgeting* 2(Suppl. 1).

Tanzi, Vito, and Schuknecht, Ludger. 2000. *Public Spending in the 20th Century—A Global Perspective.* Cambridge, U.K.: Cambridge University Press.

Wilbur, Robert H. 2000. *The Complete Guide to Nonprofit Management*, 2nd ed. New York: John Wiley & Sons.

Public Sector Performance Management

Kotler, Philip. 2002. *Strategic Marketing for Non-Profit Organizations*, 6th ed. Englewood Cliffs, New Jersey: Prentice Hall.

Niven, Paul R. 2003. *Balanced Scorecard Step-by-Step for Government and Nonprofit Agencies.* New York: John Wiley & Sons.

Osborne, David, and Peter Hutchinson. 2004. *The Price of Government—Getting the Results We Need in an Age of Permanent Fiscal Crisis.* New York: Basic Books.

Poister, Theodore H. 2003. *Measuring Performance in Public and Non-Profit Organizations.* San Francisco: Jossey-Bass

Popovich, Mark G. 1998. *Creating High-Performance Government Organizations—A Practical Guide for Public Managers.* San Francisco: Jossey-Bass
Smith, Peter. 1996. *Measuring Outcome in the Public Sector.* London: Taylor & Francis.
Wholey, Joseph S., Harry P. Hatry, and Kathryn E. Newcomer. 2004. *Handbook of Practical Program Evaluation.* San Francisco: Jossey-Bass.

Corporate Strategy

Grant, Robert M. 2002. *Contemporary Strategy Analysis—Concepts, Techniques and Applications,* 4th ed. Oxford, U.K.: Blackwell.
Johnson, Gerry, and Kevan Scholes. 2002. *Exploring Corporate Strategy,* 6th ed. Harlow, Essex, U.K.: Financial Times/Prentice Hall.
Porter, Michael E. 1998. *Competitive Advantage.* New York: The Free Press.

Corporate Finance

Brealey, Richard A., and Stewart C. Myers. 2003. *Principles of Corporate Finance.* New York: McGraw-Hill.
Neale, Bill, and Trevor McAlroy. 2004. *Business Finance—A Value-Based Approach.* Harlow, Essex, U.K.: Pearson Education Ltd.
Rappaport, Alfred. 1998. *Creating Shareholder Value: A Guide for Managers and Investors.* New York: The Free Press.
Stern, Erik, and Michael Hutchinson. 2004. *The Value Mindset—Returning to the First Principles of Capitalist Enterprise.* New York: John Wiley & Sons.
Stern, Joel M., John S. Shiely, and Irwin Ross. 2003. *The EVA Challenge.* New York: John Wiley & Sons.

Corporate Performance Management

Cokins, Gary. 2004. *Performance Management—Finding the Missing Pieces to Close the Intelligence Gaps.* New York: John Wiley & Sons.
Kaplan, Robert S., and David P. Norton. 2000. *The Strategy-Focused Organization—How Balanced Scorecard Companies Thrive in the New Business Environment.* Boston: Harvard Business School Press.
Kaplan, Robert S., and David P. Norton. 2004. *Strategy Maps—Converting Intangible Assets into Tangible Outcomes.* Boston: Harvard Business School Press.

Web Sites

Accenture Institute for Public Service Value: http://www.accenture.com/publicservicevalue
Forrester Research: http://www.forrester.com
Gartner: https://www.gartner.com
Harvard University: www.hup.harvard.edu/catalog/MOOCRE.html
Heritage Foundation: http://www.heritage.org
Institute for Citizen-Centred Service: http://www.iccs-isac.org/eng/cf-about.htm
Institute for Public Policy Research: http://www.ippr.org.uk
New Zealand State Services Commission: http://www.ssc.govt.nz/display/document.asp?navid=208&docid=3528&pageno=3
Social Market Foundation: http://www.smf.co.uk
RAND: http://www.rand.org
United Kingdom—Cabinet Office: www.strategy.gov.uk/seminars/public_value/index.asp
United States—Key National Indicators Initiatives: http://www.keyindicators.org/
United States—National Performance Review "Best Practices in Performance Measurement": http://govinfo.library.unt.edu/npr/library/papers/bkgrd/balmeasure.html
United States—The Performance Based Management Handbook: http://www.orau.gov/pbm/pbmhandbook/pbmhandbook.html
The Work Foundation: http://www.theworkfoundation.com/research/public_value.jsp

About the Authors

Martin (Marty) Cole
Group Chief Executive—Government
Accenture

Mr. Cole is Group Chief Executive of Accenture's global Government operating group, a position to which he was appointed in September 2004. He is a member of Accenture's Executive Leadership Team.

The Government group is one of the five primary business lines for Accenture. The group operates in 25 countries serving national, state/provincial and local governments. Mr. Cole is involved directly with many of the strategic initiatives undertaken by the practice.

Prior to being appointed to his current position, Mr. Cole was global managing partner of Accenture's Outsourcing & Infrastructure Delivery group, where he led the development and oversaw the execution of Accenture's transformational outsourcing strategy. In that position he had overall responsibility for the global delivery capability of a wide variety of outsourcing services, including technology infrastructure, applications and business process outsourcing. Mr. Cole was also a leader in the strategic development and deployment of Accenture's global sourcing approach and oversaw the expansion of the company's network of multiclient business process outsourcing delivery capabilities.

Mr. Cole was profiled in the April 2004 issue of *Consulting* magazine as one of the IT industry's top six power brokers. He was also a recipient of the 2002 ComputerWorld Top 100 IT Leaders award. Prior to serving as managing partner of Accenture's Outsourcing & Infrastructure Delivery group, Mr. Cole held numerous leadership positions in Accenture's Government operating group, including Managing Partner of New Business Models, Operating Unit Managing Partner for State and Local Government in North America and Managing Partner for the Northeast and East geographic regions.

Mr. Cole joined Accenture in 1980 in the Austin, Texas, office and became a partner in 1989. He was transferred to the Hartford, Connecticut, office in 1992. He still resides in Connecticut. He currently serves as a member of the Board of Trustees for Avon Old Farms School in Avon, Connecticut.

Born and raised in Chicago, Mr. Cole received his undergraduate degree from Dartmouth College in 1978 and a master of public affairs degree from the University of Texas in 1980.

Greg Parston
Director
Accenture Institute for Public Service Value

Greg Parston is the Director of the Accenture Institute for Public Service Value. Prior to joining Accenture, Dr. Parston was the Chairman of the Office for Public Management, a nonprofit organizational development company, which he co-founded in 1988 and led as Chief Executive until 2003. From 2004, Dr. Parston was also on the management board of the Priory Group, Europe's largest independent provider of mental health and specialist education services, where he was Director of Public Service Partnerships.

Dr. Parston has consulted widely with top managers, focusing on governance, leadership, strategy and change. He has worked as a senior manager in all three sectors: public, private and nonprofit. He was Deputy Director of the King's Fund College in London, Vice President of Planning and Development at Downstate Medical Center in New York City and Director of Planning for the Ottawa Regional Health Council.

Born in Detroit, Dr. Parston was educated in architecture and economics at the University of Michigan and earned a PhD in 1977 at the University of London as a Marshall Scholar. He has been on the faculty of New York University and of the King's Fund College in London and a visiting lecturer at Harvard University's John F. Kennedy School of Government. He was awarded the Operational Research Society's Goodeve Medal for distinguished contribution to literature and has twice received the European Healthcare Management Association's award for innovation in management development.

Dr. Parston has served on Her Majesty's Treasury's Public Sector Productivity Panel since 2000, and co-authored the Panel's reports on motivation and performance and on accountability. Recently, he chaired the Barrow-Cadbury Trust's Commission on Young Adults and the Criminal Justice System. Among other appointments, he was a member of the Independent Commission on Good Governance in Public Services, the Association of Chief Executive of Voluntary Organisation's Commission on the Role of the Voluntary Sector in Public Services, and the Cabinet Office's Advisory Group on Strengthening Leadership in the Public Sector. He is a trustee of the English Touring Theatre. He lives in London and Tucson.

Index